FACTS ABOUT
ISRAEL

1996

TABLE OF CONTENTS

history

Biblical Times   10

Foreign Domination   15

The State of Israel   32

Historical Highlights   48

the state

Political Structure   59

The Presidency   60

Legislature: The Knesset   61

Executive: The Government   63

The Judiciary   67

Local Government   71

Israel Defense Forces (IDF)   73

land and people

The Land   79

Nature   86

Infrastructure   91

Urban Life   96

Rural Life   103

society

Jewish Society   108

Minority Communities   118

Religious Freedom   123

health and social services

Health Services   130

Medical Research   136

Environmental Hazards   138

Sharing Beyond Borders   140

Social Services   142

Social Insurance   146

Voluntary Services   148

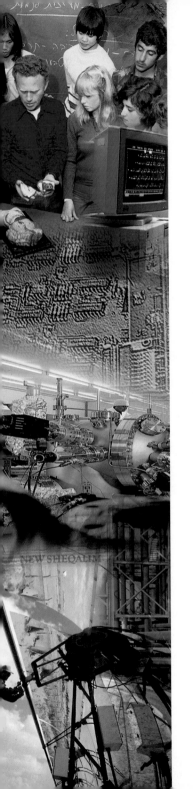

education

Challenges   152

Preschool Education   154

School System   155

Secondary Education   158

Higher Education   160

Adult Education   167

Sports   168

science and technology

Beginnings   174

Professional Personnel   175

Research and Development (R&D)   176

Worldwide Ties   187

economy

Four Challenges   192

The Balance of Payments   194

An Economic Picture   197

Economic Sectors   202

culture

Literature   214

Fine Arts   229

Museums   238

Music   242

Dance   248

Theater   253

Cinema   257

Light Entertainment   260

Media   261

israel among the nations

North America   268

Latin America   271

Europe   272

Africa   274

Asia and the Pacific   275

Arab Countries   276

The Holy See   281

International Cooperation   282

United Nations   284

World Jewry   285

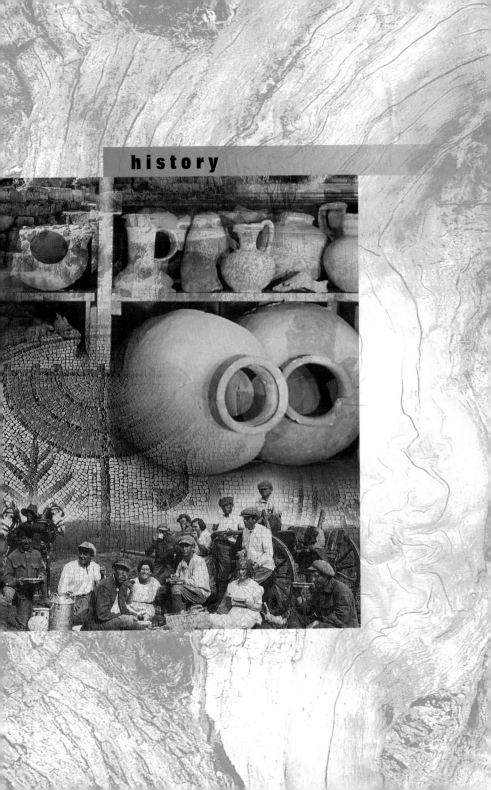

HISTORY

BIBLICAL TIMES

FOREIGN DOMINATION

THE STATE OF ISRAEL

HISTORICAL HIGHLIGHTS

זכר ימות עולם בינו שנות דור דור...
(דברים ל"ב: ז')

Remember the days of old,
consider the years of ages past....
(Deuteronomy 32:7)

The birthplace of the Jewish people is the Land of Israel (*Eretz Israel*). There, a significant part of the nation's long history was enacted, of which the first thousand years are recorded in the Bible; there, its cultural, religious and national identity was formed; and there, its physical presence has been maintained through the centuries, even after the majority was forced into exile. During the many years of dispersion, the Jewish people never severed nor forgot its bond with the Land. With the establishment of the State of Israel in 1948, Jewish independence, lost two thousand years earlier, was renewed.

BIBLICAL TIMES
THE PATRIARCHS

Jewish history began about 4,000 years ago (c. 17th century BCE) with the patriarchs – Abraham, his son Isaac and grandson Jacob. Documents unearthed in Mesopotamia, dating back to 2000 – 1500 BCE, corroborate aspects of their nomadic way of life as described in the Bible. The Book of Genesis relates how Abraham was summoned from Ur of the Chaldeans to Canaan to bring about the formation of a people with belief in the One God. When a famine spread through Canaan, Jacob (Israel), his twelve sons and their families settled in Egypt, where their descendants were reduced to slavery and pressed into forced labor.

EXODUS AND SETTLEMENT

After 400 years of bondage, the Israelites were led to freedom by Moses who, according to the biblical narrative, was chosen by God to take his people out of Egypt and back to the Land of Israel promised to their forefathers (c. 13th-12th centuries BCE). They wandered for 40 years in the Sinai desert, where they were forged into a nation and received the *Torah* (Pentateuch), which included the Ten Commandments and gave form and content to their monotheistic faith. The exodus from Egypt (c.1300 BCE) left an indelible imprint on the national memory of the Jewish people and became a universal symbol of liberty and freedom. Every year Jews celebrate *Pesach* (Passover), *Shavuot* (Pentecost) and *Succot* (Feast of Tabernacles), commemorating events of that time.

During the next two centuries, the Israelites conquered most of the Land of Israel and relinquished their nomadic ways to become farmers and craftsmen; a degree of economic and social consolidation followed. Periods of relative peace alternated with times of war during which the people rallied behind leaders known as 'judges,' chosen for their political and military skills as well as for their leadership qualities. The weakness inherent in this tribal organization in face of a threat posed by the Philistines (sea-going people from Asia Minor who settled on the country's Mediterranean coast) generated the need for a ruler who would unite the tribes and make the position permanent, with succession carried on by inheritance.

THE MONARCHY

The first king, Saul (c. 1020 BCE), bridged the period between loose tribal organization and the setting up of a full monarchy under his successor, David.

King David (c.1004–965 BCE) established Israel as a major power in the region by successful military expeditions, including the final defeat of the Philistines, as well as through a network of friendly alliances with nearby kingdoms. Consequently, his authority was recognized from the borders of Egypt and the Red Sea to the banks of the Euphrates. At home, he united the twelve Israelite tribes into one kingdom and placed his capital, Jerusalem, and the monarchy at the center of the country's national life. Biblical tradition describes David as a poet and musician, with verses ascribed to him appearing in the Book of Psalms.

David was succeeded by his son Solomon (c.965–930 BCE) who further strengthened the kingdom. Through treaties with neighboring kings, reinforced by politically motivated marriages, Solomon ensured peace for his kingdom and made it equal among the great powers of the age. He expanded foreign trade and promoted domestic prosperity by developing major enterprises such as copper mining and metal smelting, while building new towns and fortifying old ones of strategic and economic importance. Crowning his achievements was the building of the Temple in Jerusalem, which became the center of the Jewish people's national and religious life. The Bible attributes to Solomon the Book of Proverbs and the Song of Songs.

DIVIDED MONARCHY

The end of Solomon's rule was marred by discontent on the part of the populace, which had to pay heavily for his ambitious schemes. At the same time, preferential treatment of his own tribe embittered the others, which resulted in growing antagonism between the monarchy and the tribal separatists. After Solomon's death (930 BCE), open insurrection led to the breaking away of the ten northern tribes and division of the country into a northern kingdom, Israel, and a southern kingdom, Judah, on the territory of the tribes of Judah and Benjamin.

The Kingdom of Israel, with its capital Samaria, lasted more than 200 years under 19 kings, while the Kingdom of Judah was ruled from Jerusalem for 350 years by an equal number of kings of the lineage of David. The expansion of the Assyrian and Babylonian empires brought first Israel and later Judah under foreign control. The Kingdom of Israel was crushed by the Assyrians (722 BCE) and its people carried off into exile and oblivion. Over a hundred years later, Babylonia conquered the Kingdom of Judah, exiling most of its inhabitants as well as destroying Jerusalem and the Temple (586 BCE).

land: *"If I forget you, O Jerusalem, let my right hand wither; let my tongue stick to my palate if I cease to think of you, if I do not keep Jerusalem in memory even at my happiest hour"* (Psalms 137:5-6).

THE FIRST EXILE (586–538 BCE)

The Babylonian conquest brought an end to the First Jewish Commonwealth (First Temple period) but did not sever the Jewish people's connection to the Land of Israel. Sitting by the rivers of Babylon, the Jews pledged to remember their homeland.

The exile to Babylonia, which followed the destruction of the First Temple (586 BCE), marked the beginning of the Jewish Diaspora. There, Judaism began to develop a religious framework and way of life outside the Land, ultimately ensuring the people's national survival and spiritual identity and imbuing it with sufficient vitality to safeguard its future as a nation.

The Prophets: Religious sages and charismatic figures, who were perceived as being endowed with a divine gift of revelation, preached during the period of the monarchy until a century after the destruction of Jerusalem (586 BCE). Whether as advisers to kings on matters of religion, ethics and politics, or as their critics, under the primacy of the relationship between the individual and God, the prophets were guided by the need for justice and issued powerful commentaries on the morality of Jewish national life. Their revelatory experiences were recorded in books of inspired prose and poetry, many of which were incorporated into the Bible.

The enduring, universal appeal of the prophets derives from their call for a fundamental consideration of human values. Words such as those of Isaiah (1:17), *"Learn to do good, devote yourselves to justice; aid the wronged, uphold the rights of the orphan; defend the cause of the widow,"* continue to nourish humanity's pursuit of social justice.

First century BCE Hasmonean coin

Stone relief on Arch of Titus in Rome, first century

Gold-leaf decoration on 4th century glass bowl found in Rome

Menorah from the emblem of the State of Israel

THE MENORAH THROUGH THE AGES

The Golden Menorah (a seven-branched candelabrum) was a major ritual object in King Solomon's Temple in ancient Jerusalem. Through the ages it has served as a symbol of Jewish heritage and tradition in countless places and in a variety of forms.

FOREIGN DOMINATION
PERSIAN AND HELLENISTIC PERIODS (538–142 BCE)

Following a decree by the Persian King Cyrus, conqueror of the Babylonian empire (538 BCE), some 50,000 Jews set out on the First Return to the Land of Israel, led by Zerubabel, a descendant of the House of David. Less than a century later, the Second Return was led by Ezra the Scribe. Over the next four centuries, the Jews knew varying degrees of self-rule under Persian (538–333 BCE) and later Hellenistic (Ptolemaic and Seleucid) overlordship (332–142 BCE).

The repatriation of the Jews under Ezra's inspired leadership, construction of the Second Temple on the site of the First Temple, refortification of Jerusalem's walls and establishment of the *Knesset Hagedolah* (Great Assembly) as the supreme religious and judicial body of the Jewish people marked the beginning of the Second Jewish Commonwealth (Second Temple period). Within the confines of the Persian Empire, Judah was a nation centered in Jerusalem whose leadership was entrusted to the high priest and council of elders.

As part of the ancient world conquered by Alexander the Great (332 BCE) of Greece, the Land remained a Jewish theocracy under Syrian-based Seleucid rulers. When the Jews were prohibited from practicing Judaism and their Temple was desecrated as part of an effort to impose Greek-oriented culture and customs on the entire population, the Jews rose in revolt (166 BCE). First led by Mattathias of the priestly Hasmonean family and then by his son Judah the Maccabee, the Jews subsequently entered Jerusalem and purified the Temple (164 BCE), events commemorated each year by the festival of Hanukkah.

HASMONEAN DYNASTY (142–63 BCE)

Following further Hasmonean victories (147 BCE), the Seleucids restored autonomy to Judea, as the Land of Israel was now called, and, with the collapse of the Seleucid kingdom (129 BCE), Jewish independence was again achieved. Under the Hasmonean dynasty, which lasted about 80 years, the kingdom regained boundaries not far short of Solomon's realm, political consolidation under Jewish rule was attained and Jewish life flourished.

ROMAN RULE (63 BCE–313 CE)

When the Romans replaced the Seleucids as the great power in the region, they granted the Hasmonean king, Hyrcanus II, limited authority

Model of the Second Temple

Judea by the Romans. Granted almost unlimited autonomy in the country's internal affairs, he became one of the most powerful monarchs in the eastern part of the Roman Empire. A great admirer of Greco-Roman culture, Herod launched a massive construction program, which included the cities of Caesarea and Sebaste and the fortresses at Herodium and Masada. He also remodeled the Temple into one of the most magnificent buildings of its time. But despite his many achievements, Herod failed to win the trust and support of his Jewish subjects.

Ten years after Herod's death (4 BCE), Judea came under direct Roman administration. Growing anger against increased Roman suppression of Jewish life resulted in sporadic violence which esclated into a full-scale revolt in 66 CE. Superior Roman forces led by Titus were finally victorious, razing Jerusalem to the ground (70 CE) and defeating the last Jewish outpost at Masada (73 CE).

under the Roman governor of Damascus. The Jews were hostile to the new regime, and the following years witnessed frequent insurrections. A last attempt to restore the former glory of the Hasmonean dynasty was made by Mattathias Antigonus, whose defeat and death brought Hasmonean rule to an end (40 BCE), and the Land became a province of the Roman Empire.

In 37 BCE Herod, a son-in-law of Hyrcanus II, was appointed King of

The total destruction of Jerusalem and the Temple was catastrophic for the Jewish people. According to the contemporary historian Josephus Flavius, hundreds of thousands of Jews perished in the siege of Jerusalem and elsewhere in the country, and many thousands more were sold into slavery.

Masada: Nearly 1,000 Jewish men, women and children, who had survived the destruction of Jerusalem, occupied and fortified King Herod's mountaintop palace complex of Masada near the Dead Sea, where they held out for three years against repeated Roman attempts to dislodge them. When the Romans finally scaled Masada and broke through its walls, they found that the defenders and their families had chosen to die by their own hands rather than be enslaved. In recent years, Masada has become a symbol of the Jewish people's determination to be free in its own land.

A last brief period of Jewish sovereignty in ancient times followed the revolt of Shimon Bar Kokhba (132 CE), during which Jerusalem and Judea were regained. However, given the overwhelming power of the Romans, the outcome was inevitable. Three years later, in conformity with Roman custom, Jerusalem was *"plowed up with a yoke of oxen,"* Judea was renamed *Palaestina* and Jerusalem, *Aelia Capitolina*.

Although the Temple had been destroyed and Jerusalem burned to the ground, the Jews and Judaism survived the encounter with Rome. The supreme legislative and judicial body, the *Sanhedrin* (successor of the *Knesset Hagedolah*) was reconvened in Yavneh (70 CE), and later in Tiberias. Without the unifying framework of a state and the Temple, the small remaining Jewish community gradually recovered, reinforced from time to time by returning exiles. Institutional and communal life was renewed, priests were replaced by rabbis and the synagogue became the focus of Jewish settlement, as evidenced by remnants of synagogues found at Capernaum, Korazin, Bar'am, Gamla and elsewhere. *Halakhah* (Jewish religious law) served as the common bond among the Jews and was passed on from generation to generation.

First century synagogue at Katzrin

Halakhah is the body of law which has guided Jewish life all over the world since post-biblical times. It deals with the religious obligations of Jews, both in interpersonal relations and in ritual observances, and encompasses practically all aspects of human behavior – birth and marriage, joy and grief, agriculture and commerce, ethics and theology. Rooted in the Bible, halakhic authority is based on the *Talmud*, a body of Jewish law and lore (completed c. 400), which incorporates the *Mishnah*, the first written compilation of the Oral Law (codified c. 210), and the *Gemarah*, an elaboration of the Mishnah. To provide practical guidance to the Halakhah, concise, systematic digests were authored by religious scholars beginning in the first and second centuries. Among the most authoritative of these codifications is the *Shulhan Arukh*, written by Joseph Caro in Safed (*Tzfat*) in the 16th century.

Byzantine Rule (313–636)

By the end of the 4th century, following Emperor Constantine's conversion to Christianity (313) and the founding of the Byzantine Empire, the Land of Israel had become a predominantly Christian country. Churches were built on Christian holy sites in Jerusalem, Bethlehem and Galilee, and monasteries were established in many parts of the country. Jews were deprived of their former relative autonomy, as well as of their right to hold public positions, and were forbidden to enter Jerusalem except on one day of the year (*Tisha b'Av* – ninth of Av) to mourn the destruction of the Temple.

The Persian invasion of 614 was aided by the Jews, who were inspired by messianic hopes of deliverance. In gratitude for their help, they were granted the administration of Jerusalem, an interlude which lasted about three years. Subsequently, the Byzantine army regained the city (629) and again expelled its Jewish inhabitants.

Arab Rule (636–1099)

The Arab conquest of the Land came four years after the death of the prophet Muhammad (632) and lasted more than four centuries, with caliphs ruling first from Damascus, then from Baghdad and Egypt. At the outset, Jewish settlement in Jerusalem resumed, and the Jewish community was granted the customary protected status of non-Muslims under Islamic rule, which safeguarded their lives, property and freedom of worship in return for payment of special poll and land taxes.

However, subsequent restrictions against non-Muslims (717) affected the Jews' public conduct as well as their religious observances and legal status. The imposition of heavy taxes on agricultural land compelled many to move from rural areas to towns, where their circumstances hardly improved, while increasing social and economic discrimination forced others to leave the country. By the end of the 11th century, the Jewish community in the Land had diminished considerably and had lost some of its organizational and religious cohesiveness.

THE CRUSADERS (1099–1291)

For the next 200 years, the country was dominated by the Crusaders who, following an appeal by Pope Urban II, came from Europe to recover the Holy Land from the infidels. In July 1099, after a five-week siege, the knights of the First Crusade and their rabble army captured Jerusalem, massacring most of the city's non-Christian inhabitants. Barricaded in their synagogues, the Jews defended their quarter, only to be burned to death or sold into slavery. During the next few decades, the Crusaders extended their power over the rest of the country, partly through treaties and agreements, but mostly by bloody military victories. The Latin Kingdom of the Crusaders was that of a conquering minority confined mainly to fortified cities and castles.

When the Crusaders opened up transportation routes from Europe, pilgrimages to the Holy Land became popular and, at the same time, increasing numbers of Jews sought to return to their homeland. Documents of the period indicate that 300 rabbis from France and England arrived in a group, some settling in Acre (*Akko*), others in Jerusalem.

Following the overthrow of the Crusaders by a Muslim army under Saladin (1187), the Jews were again accorded a certain measure of freedom, including the right to live in Jerusalem. Although the Crusaders regained a foothold in the country after Saladin's death (1193), their presence was limited to a network of fortified castles. Crusader authority in the Land ended after a final defeat (1291) by the Mamluks, a Muslim military class which had come to power in Egypt.

MAMLUK RULE (1291–1516)

The Land under the Mamluks became a backwater province ruled from Damascus. Acre, Jaffa (*Yafo*) and other ports were destroyed for fear of new crusades, and maritime as well as overland commerce was interrupted. By the end of the Middle Ages, the country's towns were virtually in ruins, most of Jerusalem was abandoned and the small Jewish community was poverty-stricken. The period of Mamluk decline was darkened by political and economic upheavals, plagues, locusts and devastating earthquakes.

OTTOMAN RULE (1517–1917)

Following the Ottoman conquest in 1517, the Land was divided into four districts, attached administratively to the province of Damascus and ruled from Istanbul. At the outset of the Ottoman era, some 1,000 Jewish families lived in the country, mainly in Jerusalem, Nablus (*Shehem*), Hebron, Gaza, Safed (*Tzfat*) and the villages of Galilee. The community was comprised of descendants of Jews who had always lived in the Land, as well as immigrants from North Africa and Europe.

Orderly government, until the death (1566) of Sultan Suleiman the

Magnificent, brought improvements and stimulated Jewish immigration. Some newcomers settled in Jerusalem, but the majority went to Safed where, by the mid-16th century, the Jewish population had risen to about 10,000, and the town had become a thriving textile center as well as the focus of intense intellectual activity. During this period, the study of *Kabbalah* (Jewish mysticism) flourished, and contemporary clarifications of Jewish law, as codified in the *Shulhan Arukh*, spread throughout the Diaspora from the houses of study in Safed.

With a gradual decline in the quality of Ottoman rule, the country suffered widespread neglect. By the end of the 18th century, much of the land was owned by absentee landlords and leased to impoverished tenant farmers, and taxation was as crippling as it was capricious. The great forests of Galilee and the Carmel mountain range were denuded of trees; swamp and desert encroached on agricultural land.

The 19th century saw medieval backwardness gradually give way to the first signs of progress, with various Western powers jockeying for position, often through missionary activities. British, French and American scholars launched studies of biblical archaeology; Britain, France, Russia, Austria and the United States opened consulates in Jerusalem. Steamships began to ply regular routes between the Land and Europe; postal and telegraphic connections were installed; the first road was built connecting Jerusalem and Jaffa. The Land's rebirth as a crossroads for commerce of three continents was accelerated by the opening of the Suez Canal.

Consequently, the situation of the country's Jews slowly improved, and their numbers increased substantially. By mid-century, overcrowded conditions within the walled city of Jerusalem motivated the Jews to build the first neighborhood outside the walls (1860) and, in the next quarter century, to add seven more, forming the nucleus of the New City. By 1880, Jerusalem had an overall Jewish majority. Land for farming was purchased throughout the country; new rural settlements were established; and the Hebrew language, long restricted to liturgy and literature, was revived. The stage was set for the founding of the Zionist movement.

Inspired by Zionist ideology, two major influxes of Jews from Eastern Europe arrived in the country at the end of the 19th and the beginning of the 20th centuries. Resolved to restore their homeland by working the soil, these pioneers reclaimed barren

Zionism, the national liberation movement of the Jewish people, derives its name from the word 'Zion,' the traditional synonym for Jerusalem and the Land of Israel. The idea of Zionism – the redemption of the Jewish people in its ancestral homeland – is rooted in the continuous longing for and deep attachment to the Land of Israel, which have been an inherent part of Jewish existence in the Diaspora through the centuries.

Political Zionism emerged in response to continued oppression and persecution of Jews in Eastern Europe and increasing disillusionment with the emancipation in Western Europe, which had neither put an end to discrimination nor led to the integration of Jews into local societies. It found formal expression in the establishment of the Zionist Organization (1897) at the First Zionist Congress, convened by Theodor Herzl in Basel, Switzerland. The Zionist movement's program contained both ideological and practical elements aimed at promoting the return of Jews to the Land; facilitating the social, cultural, economic and political revival of Jewish national life; and attaining an internationally recognized, legally secured home for the Jewish people in its historic homeland, where Jews would be free from persecution and able to develop their own lives and identity.

fields, built new settlements and laid the foundations for what would become a thriving agricultural economy. The new arrivals faced extremely harsh conditions, as the attitude of the Ottoman administration was hostile and oppressive; communications and transportation were rudimentary and insecure; swamps bred deadly malaria; and the soil itself suffered from centuries of neglect. Land purchases were restricted, and construction was banned without a special permit obtainable only in Istanbul.

While these difficulties hampered the country's development, they did not stop it. At the outbreak of World War I (1914), the Jewish population in the Land numbered 85,000, as compared to 5,000 in the early 1500s.

In December 1917, British forces under the command of General Allenby entered Jerusalem, ending 400 years of Ottoman rule. The Jewish Legion, with three battalions comprising thousands of Jewish volunteers, was then an integral unit of the British army.

BRITISH RULE (1918–1948)

In July 1922, the League of Nations entrusted Great Britain with the Mandate for Palestine (the name by which the country was then known). Recognizing *"the historical connection of the Jewish people with Palestine,"* Great Britain was called upon to facilitate the establishment of a Jewish national home in Palestine–*Eretz Israel* (Land of Israel). Two months later, in September 1922, the Council of the League of Nations and Great Britain decided that the provisions for setting up a Jewish national home would not apply to the area east of the Jordan River, which constituted three fourths of the territory included in the Mandate and eventually became the Hashemite Kingdom of Jordan.

Immigration

Motivated by Zionism and encouraged by British *"sympathy with Jewish Zionist aspirations,"* as communicated

British General Allenby enters Jerusalem, 1917

by Foreign Secretary Lord Balfour (1917), successive waves of immigrants arrived in the Land between 1919 and 1939, each contributing to different aspects of the developing Jewish community. Some 35,000 who came between 1919 and 1923, mainly from Russia, strongly influenced the community's character and organization for years to come. These pioneers laid the foundations of a comprehensive social and economic infrastructure, developed agriculture, established unique communal forms of rural settlement – the *kibbutz* and *moshav* – and provided the labor force for building housing and roads. The next influx of some 60,000, which arrived primarily from Poland between 1924 and 1932, was instrumental in developing and enriching urban life. These immigrants settled mainly in Tel Aviv, Haifa and Jerusalem, where they established small businesses, construction firms and light industry. The last major wave of immigration before World War II, comprising some 165,000, took place in the 1930s following Hitler's rise to power in Germany. The newcomers, many of whom were professionals and academics, constituted the first large-scale influx from Western and Central Europe. Their education, skills and experience raised business standards, improved urban and rural amenities and broadened the community's cultural life.

Administration

The British Mandate authorities granted the Jewish and Arab communities the right to run their own internal affairs. Utilizing this right, the Jewish community, known as the *yishuv*, elected (1920) a self-governing body based on party representation, which met annually to review its activities and elect the National Council (*Vaad Leumi*) to implement its policies and programs. Financed by local resources and funds raised by world Jewry, a countrywide network of educational, religious, health and social services was developed and maintained. In 1922, as stipulated in the Mandate, a 'Jewish Agency' was constituted to represent the Jewish people vis-a-vis the British authorities, foreign governments and international organizations.

Economic Development

During the three decades of the Mandate, agriculture was expanded; factories were established; new roads were built throughout the country; the waters of the Jordan River were harnessed for production of electric power; and the mineral potential of the Dead Sea was tapped. The *Histadrut* (General Federation of Labor) was founded (1920) to advance workers' welfare and provide employment by setting up cooperatively-owned enterprises in the industrial sector as well as marketing services for the communal agricultural settlements.

Dead Sea Works, 1920s

Culture

Day by day, a cultural life was emerging which would become unique to the Jewish community in the Land of Israel. Art, music and dance developed gradually with the establishment of professional schools and studios. Galleries and halls were set up to provide venues for exhibitions and performances attended by a discriminating public. The opening of a new play, the appearance of a new book or a retrospective show by a local painter were immediately scrutinized by the press and became the subject of lively discussion in coffee shops and at social gatherings.

The Hebrew language was recognized as one of three official languages of the country, alongside English and Arabic, and was used on documents, coins and stamps, as well as for radio broadcasting. Publishing proliferated, and the country emerged as the world center of Hebrew literary activity. Theaters of various genres opened their doors to enthusiastic audiences, accompanied by first attempts to write original Hebrew plays.

Arab Opposition and British Restrictions

The Jewish national revival and the community's efforts to rebuild the country were strongly opposed by Arab nationalists. Their resentment erupted in periods of intense violence (1920, 1921, 1929, 1936–39) when Jewish transport was harassed, fields and forests set on fire, and unprovoked attacks launched against the Jewish population. Attempts to reach a dialogue with the Arabs, undertaken early in the Zionist endeavor, were ultimately unsuccessful, polarizing Zionism and Arab nationalism into a potentially explosive situation. Recognizing the opposing aims of the two national movements, the British recommended (1937) dividing the country into two states, one Jewish and one Arab. The Jewish leadership accepted the idea of partition and empowered the Jewish Agency to negotiate with the British government in an effort to reformulate some aspects of the proposal. The Arabs were uncompromisingly against any partition plan.

Continuing large-scale Arab anti-Jewish riots led Britain (May 1939) to issue a White Paper imposing drastic restrictions on Jewish immigration, despite its consequence of denying European Jewry a place of refuge from Nazi persecution. The start of World War II soon after caused David Ben-Gurion, later Israel's first prime minister, to declare: "*We will fight the war as if there were no White Paper, and the White Paper as if there were no war.*"

Three Jewish underground movements operated during the British Mandate period. The largest was the *Haganah*, founded in 1920 by the Jewish community as a defense militia to safeguard the security of the Jewish population. From the mid-1930s, it also retaliated following Arab attacks and responded to British restrictions on Jewish immigration with mass demonstrations and sabotage. The *Etzel*, organized in 1931, rejected the self-restraint of the Haganah and initiated independent actions against both Arab and British targets. The smallest and most militant group, the *Lehi*, set up in 1940, was motivated mainly by its anti-British attitude. The three organizations were disbanded with the establishment of the Israel Defense Forces in May 1948.

Jewish volunteers in World War II: Over 26,000 men and women of the Jewish community in the Land volunteered to join the British forces in the fight against Nazi Germany and its Axis allies, serving in the army, air force and navy. In September 1944, following a prolonged effort by the Jewish Agency in the country and the Zionist movement abroad to achieve recognition of the participation of the Jews of Palestine in the war effort, the Jewish Brigade was formed as an independent military unit of the British army, with its own flag and emblem. Comprised of some 5,000 men, the Brigade saw action in Egypt, northern Italy and northwest Europe. After the Allied victory in Europe (1945), many of its members joined the 'illegal immigration' efforts to bring Holocaust survivors to the Land of Israel.

The Holocaust

During World War II (1939–45), the Nazi regime deliberately carried out a systematic master plan to liquidate the Jewish community of Europe, in the course of which some six million Jews, including 1.5 million children, were murdered. As the Nazi armies swept through Europe, Jews were savagely persecuted, subjected to every conceivable torture and humiliation, and herded into ghettos where attempts at armed resistance led to even harsher measures. From the ghettos they were transported to camps where a fortunate few were put to hard labor, but most were either shot in mass executions or put to death in gas chambers. Not many managed to escape. Some fled to other countries, a few joined the partisans and others were hidden by non-Jews who did so at risk of their own lives. Consequently, only one third, including those who had left Europe before the war, survived out of a population of almost nine million, which had once constituted the largest and most vibrant Jewish community in the world.

After the war, the British intensified their restrictions on the number of Jews permitted to enter and settle in the Land. The Jewish community responded by instituting a wide network of "illegal immigration" activities to rescue Holocaust survivors. Between 1945 and 1948, some 85,000 Jews were brought to the Land by secret, often dangerous routes, in spite of a British naval blockade and border patrols set up to intercept the refugees before they reached the country. Those who were caught were interned in detention camps on the island of Cyprus.

Yad Vashem, *Holocaust memorial*

Flag of Israel to be raised at the United Nations, 1949

ROAD TO INDEPENDENCE

Britain's inability to reconcile the conflicting demands of the Jewish and Arab communities led the British government to request that the 'Question of Palestine' be placed on the agenda of the United Nations General Assembly (April 1947). As a result, a special committee was constituted to draft proposals concerning the country's future. On 29 November 1947, the Assembly voted to adopt the committee's recommendation to partition the Land into two states, one Jewish and one Arab. The Jewish community accepted the plan; the Arabs rejected it.

Following the UN vote, local Arab militants, aided by irregular volunteers from Arab countries, launched violent attacks against the Jewish community in an effort to frustrate the partition resolution and prevent the establishment of a Jewish state. After a number of setbacks, the Jewish defense organizations routed most of the attacking forces, taking hold of the entire area which had been allocated for the Jewish state.

On 14 May 1948 when the British Mandate came to an end, the Jewish population in the Land numbered some 650,000, comprising an organized community with well-developed political, social and economic institutions – in fact, a nation in every sense and a state in everything but name.

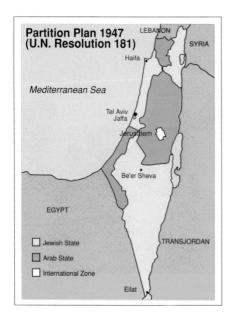

Partition Plan 1947 (U.N. Resolution 181)

LEBANON
SYRIA
Haifa
Mediterranean Sea
Tel Aviv
Jaffa
Jerusalem
Be'er Sheva
EGYPT
TRANSJORDAN
Eilat

☐ Jewish State
☐ Arab State
☐ International Zone

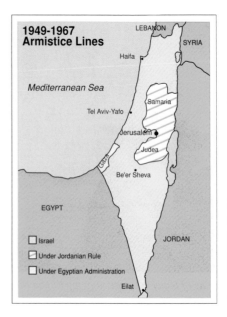

1949-1967 Armistice Lines

LEBANON
SYRIA
Haifa
Mediterranean Sea
Samaria
Tel Aviv-Yafo
Jerusalem
Judea
Be'er Sheva
EGYPT
JORDAN
Eilat

☐ Israel
☑ Under Jordanian Rule
☐ Under Egyptian Administration

THE STATE OF ISRAEL

On 14 May 1948 the State of Israel was proclaimed according to the UN partition plan (1947). Less than 24 hours later, the regular armies of Egypt, Jordan, Syria, Lebanon and Iraq invaded the country, forcing Israel to defend the sovereignty it had regained in its ancestral homeland. In what became known as Israel's War of Independence, the newly formed, poorly equipped Israel Defense Forces (IDF) repulsed the invaders in fierce intermittent fighting, which lasted some 15 months and claimed over 6,000 Israeli lives (nearly one percent of the country's Jewish population at the time).

During the first few months of 1949, direct negotiations were conducted under UN auspices between Israel and each of the invading countries (except Iraq which has refused to negotiate with Israel to date), resulting in armistice agreements which reflected the situation at the end of the fighting. Accordingly, the coastal plain, Galilee and the entire Negev were within Israel's sovereignty, Judea and Samaria (the West Bank) came under Jordanian rule, the Gaza Strip came under Egyptian administration, and the city of Jerusalem was divided, with Jordan controlling the eastern part, including the Old City, and Israel the western sector.

STATE-BUILDING

The war over, Israel focused on building the state which the people had struggled so long and so hard to regain. The first 120-seat *Knesset* (parliament) went into session following national elections (25 January 1949) in which nearly 85 percent of all eligible voters cast their ballots. Two of the people who had led Israel to statehood became the country's leaders: David Ben-Gurion, head of the Jewish Agency, was chosen as the first prime minister; and Chaim Weizmann, head of the World Zionist Organization, was elected by the Knesset as the first president. On 11 May 1949, Israel took its seat as the 59th member of the United Nations.

In accordance with the concept of the 'ingathering of the exiles' which lies at the heart of Israel's *raison d'être*, the gates of the country were thrown open, affirming the right of every Jew to come to the country and, upon entry, to acquire citizenship. In the first four months of independence, some 50,000 newcomers, mainly Holocaust survivors, reached Israel's shores. By the end of 1951, a total of 687,000 men, women and children had arrived, over 300,000 of them refugees from Arab lands, thus doubling the Jewish population.

The economic strain caused by the War of Independence and the need to provide for a rapidly growing population required austerity at home and financial aid from abroad. Assistance extended by the United States government, loans from American banks, contributions of diaspora Jews

David Ben-Gurion, man of vision

and postwar German reparations were used to build housing, mechanize agriculture, establish a merchant fleet and a national airline, exploit available minerals, develop industries and expand roads, telecommunications and electricity networks.

Towards the end of the first decade, the output of industry doubled as did the number of employed persons, with industrial exports increasing four-fold. Vast expansion of areas under cultivation had brought about self-sufficiency in the supply of all basic food products except meat and grains, while some 50,000 acres (20,000 hectares) of mostly barren land were afforested and trees were planted along almost 500 miles (800 km.) of highway.

The educational system, which had been developed by the Jewish community in the pre-state period and now included the Arab sector, was greatly expanded. School attendance became free and compulsory for all children aged 5–14 (since 1978 it has been mandatory to age 16 and free to age 18). Cultural and artistic activity flourished, blending Middle Eastern, North African and Western elements, as Jews arriving from all parts of the world brought with them the unique traditions of their own communities as well as aspects of the culture prevailing in the countries where they had lived for generations.

When Israel celebrated its 10th anniversary, the population numbered over two million.

1956 SINAI CAMPAIGN

However, the years of state-building were overshadowed by serious security problems. The 1948 armistice agreements had not only failed to pave the way to permanent peace, but were also constantly violated. In contradiction to the UN Security Council resolution of 1 September 1951, Israeli and Israel-bound shipping was prevented from passing through the Suez Canal; the blockade of the Straits of Tiran was tightened; incursions into Israel of terrorist squads from neighboring Arab countries for murder and sabotage occurred with increasing frequency; and the Sinai peninsula was gradually converted into a huge Egyptian military base.

Upon the signing of a tripartate military alliance by Egypt, Syria and Jordan (October 1956), the imminent threat to Israel's existence was intensified. In the course of an eight-day campaign, the IDF captured the Gaza Strip and the entire Sinai peninsula, halting 10 miles (16 km.) east of the Suez Canal. A United Nations decision to station a UN Emergency Force (UNEF) along the Egypt-Israel border and Egyptian assurances of free navigation in the Gulf of Eilat led Israel to agree to withdraw in stages (November 1956 – March 1957) from the areas taken a few weeks earlier.

Consequently, the Straits of Tiran were opened, enabling the development of trade with Asian and East African countries as well as oil imports from the Persian Gulf.

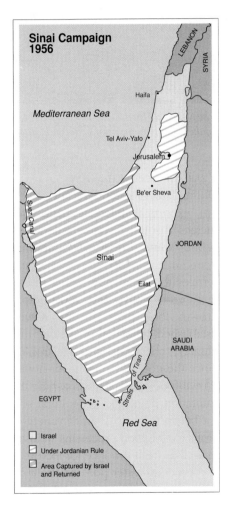

The National Water Carrier, (completed 1964), which brings water from the north and center of the country to the semi-arid south, during construction

YEARS OF CONSOLIDATION

During Israel's second decade (1958–68), exports doubled, and the GNP increased some 10 percent annually. While some previously imported items such as paper, tires, radios and refrigerators were now being manufactured locally, the most rapid growth took place in the newly-established branches of metals, machinery, chemicals and electronics. Since the domestic market for home-grown food was fast approaching the saturation point, the agricultural sector began to grow a larger variety of crops for the food processing industry as well as fresh produce for export. A second deep-water port was built on the Mediterranean coast at Ashdod, in addition to the existing one at Haifa, to handle the increased volume of trade.

In Jerusalem, a permanent home for the Knesset was built, and facilities for the Hadassah Medical Center and Hebrew University were constructed on alternate sites to replace the original buildings on Mount Scopus, which had to be abandoned after the War of Independence. At the same time, the Israel Museum was established with the aim of collecting, conserving, studying and exhibiting the cultural and artistic treasures of the Jewish people.

Israel's foreign relations expanded steadily, as close ties were developed with the United States, British

> **The Eichmann Trial:** In May 1960, Adolf Eichmann, one of the main organizers of the Nazi extermination program during World War II, was brought to the country to stand trial under Israel's Nazis and Nazi Collaborators (Punishment) Law (1950). In the trial, which opened in April 1961, Eichmann was found guilty of crimes against humanity and the Jewish people, and sentenced to death. His appeal to the Supreme Court was rejected, and he was hanged on 30 May 1962. This was the only time that the death penalty has been carried out under Israeli law.

Commonwealth countries, most western European states, nearly all the countries of Latin America and Africa, and some in Asia. Extensive programs of international cooperation were initiated, as hundreds of Israeli physicians, engineers, teachers, agronomists, irrigation experts and youth organizers shared their know-how and experience with people in other developing countries. In 1965 ambassadors were exchanged with the Federal Republic of Germany, a move which had been delayed until then because of the Jewish people's bitter memories of the crimes committed against them during the Nazi regime (1933-45). Vehement opposition and public debate preceded normalization of relations between the two countries.

The Israel Museum

1967 SIX-DAY WAR

Hopes for another decade of relative tranquillity were dashed with the escalation of Arab terrorist raids across the Egyptian and Jordanian borders, persistent Syrian artillery bombardment of agricultural settlements in northern Galilee and massive military build-ups by the neighboring Arab states. When Egypt again moved large numbers of troops into the Sinai desert (May 1967), ordered the UN peacekeeping forces (deployed since 1957) out of the area, reimposed the blockade of the Straits of Tiran and entered into a military alliance with Jordan, Israel found itself faced by hostile Arab armies on all fronts. As Egypt had violated the arrangements agreed upon following the 1956 Sinai Campaign, Israel invoked its inherent right of self-defense, launching a preemptive strike (5 June 1967) against Egypt in the south, followed by a counterattack against Jordan in the east and the routing of Syrian forces entrenched on the Golan Heights in the north.

At the end of six days of fighting, previous cease-fire lines were replaced by new ones, with Judea, Samaria, Gaza, the Sinai peninsula and the Golan Heights under Israel's control. As a result, the northern villages were freed from 19 years of recurrent Syrian shelling; the passage of Israeli and Israel-bound shipping through the Straits of Tiran was ensured; and Jerusalem, which had been divided under Israeli and Jordanian rule since 1949, was reunified under Israel's authority.

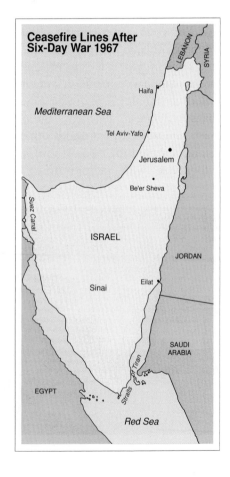

Ceasefire Lines After Six-Day War 1967

FROM WAR TO WAR

The war over, Israel's diplomatic challenge was to translate its military gains into a permanent peace based on UN Security Council Resolution 242, which called for *"acknowledgment of the sovereignty, territorial integrity and political independence of every state in the area and their right to live in peace within secure and recognized boundaries free from threats or acts of force."* However, the Arab position, as formulated at the Khartoum Summit (August 1967) called for *"no peace with Israel, no negotiations with Israel and no recognition of Israel."* In September 1968, Egypt initiated a 'war of attrition,' with sporadic, static actions along the banks of the Suez Canal, which escalated into full-scale, localized fighting, causing heavy casualties on both sides. Hostilities ended in 1970 when Egypt and Israel accepted a renewed cease-fire along the Suez Canal.

1973 YOM KIPPUR WAR

Three years of relative calm along the borders were shattered on Yom Kippur (Day of Atonement), the holiest day of the Jewish year, when Egypt and Syria launched a coordinated surprise assault against Israel (6 October 1973), with the Egyptian army crossing the Suez Canal and Syrian troops penetrating the Golan Heights.

During the next three weeks, the Israel Defense Forces turned the tide of battle and repulsed the attackers, crossing the Suez Canal into Egypt and advancing to within 20 miles (32 km.) of the Syrian capital, Damascus. Two years of difficult negotiations between Israel and Egypt and between Israel and Syria resulted in disengagement agreements, according to which Israel withdrew from parts of the territories captured during the war.

FROM WAR TO PEACE

While the 1973 war cost Israel a year's GNP, by the second half of 1974 the economy had recovered. Foreign investments grew considerably and, with Israel becoming an associate member of the European Common Market (1975), new potential outlets opened up for Israeli goods. Tourism began to increase and the annual number of visitors passed the one million mark.

The 1977 Knesset elections brought the Likud bloc, a coalition of liberal and centrist parties, to power, ending almost 30 years of Labor party dominance. Upon taking office, the new prime minister, Menachem Begin, reiterated the commitment of all previous prime ministers to strive for permanent peace in the region and called upon the Arab leaders to come to the negotiating table.

The cycle of Arab rejections of Israel's appeals for peace was broken with the visit of Egyptian President Anwar Sadat to Jerusalem (November 1977), followed by negotiations between Egypt and Israel under American auspices. The resulting Camp David Accords (September 1978) contained a framework for a comprehensive peace in the Middle East, including a detailed proposal for self-government for the Palestinians. On 26 March 1979, Israel and Egypt signed a peace treaty in Washington, DC, bringing the 30-year state of war between them to an end. In accordance with the terms of the treaty, Israel withdrew from the Sinai peninsula, exchanging former cease-fire lines and armistice agreements for mutually recognized international boundaries.

Some of the African states which had severed ties with Israel as a result of Arab pressure during the 1973 oil crisis, restored contacts in the 1980s, giving renewed momentum to economic relations, as well as reestablishing formal diplomatic ties.

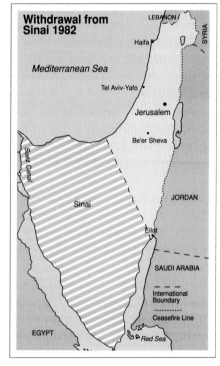

Withdrawal from Sinai 1982

Residents of northern Israel in shelters, escaping frequent bombardments

1982 OPERATION PEACE FOR GALILEE

The international boundary line with Lebanon has never been challenged by either side. However, when the Palestine Liberation Organization (PLO) redeployed itself in southern Lebanon after being expelled from Jordan (1970) and perpetrated repeated terrorist actions against the towns and villages of northern Israel (Galilee), which caused many casualties and much damage, the Israel Defense Forces crossed the border into Lebanon (1982). "Operation Peace for Galilee" resulted in removing the bulk of the PLO's organizational and military infrastructure from the area. Since then, Israel has maintained a small security zone in southern Lebanon adjacent to its northern border to safeguard its population in Galilee against continued attacks by hostile elements.

DOMESTIC CHALLENGES

During the 1980s and 1990s, Israel has absorbed over 700,000 new immigrants, mainly from the former Soviet Union, Eastern Europe and Ethiopia. The influx of so many new consumers as well as a large number of skilled and unskilled workers, coupled with strident measures to control inflation, boosted the economy into a period of accelerated expansion, attaining one of the highest GDP growth rates among Western countries.

The government which came into power after the 1984 Knesset elections was made up of the two major political blocs – Labor (left/center) and Likud (right/center). It was replaced in 1988 by a Likud-led coalition, which at the end of its four-year term was followed in 1992 by a coalition of Labor and smaller left-of-center parties. During these years, each government worked towards the achievement of peace, economic development and immigrant absorption according to its own political convictions.

TOWARDS PEACE IN THE REGION

Since the signing of the Egypt-Israel peace treaty (1979), various initiatives were put forth by Israel and others to further the peace process in the Middle East. These efforts eventually led to the convening of the Madrid Peace Conference (October 1991), held under American and Soviet auspices, which brought together representatives of Israel, Syria, Lebanon, Jordan and the Palestinians. The formal proceedings were followed by bilateral negotiations between the parties and by multilateral talks addressing regional concerns.

Bilateral Talks

Israel and the Palestinians: Following months of intensive behind-the-scenes contacts in Oslo between negotiators for Israel and the Palestine Liberation Organization (PLO), a Declaration of Principles (DOP) was formulated outlining self-government arrangements for the Palestinians in the West Bank and Gaza Strip. Its signing was preceded by an exchange of letters (September 1993) between PLO Chairman Yasser Arafat and Prime Minister Yitzhak Rabin, in which the PLO renounced the use of terrorism, pledged to invalidate those articles in its Covenant which deny Israel's right to exist and committed itself to a peaceful resolution of the decades-long conflict between the Palestinians and the Jews over the Land. In response, Israel recognized the PLO as the representative of the Palestinian people.

Signed by Israel and the PLO in Washington, DC in September 1993, the DOP contains a set of mutually agreed-upon general principles regarding a five-year interim period of Palestinian self-rule, to be implemented in four stages. The first step, setting up self-rule in the Gaza Strip and Jericho area, took place in May 1994. In August of the same year, the second stage was introduced involving the transfer of powers and responsibilities to Palestinian representatives in the West Bank through early empowerment in five specific spheres – education and culture, health, social welfare, direct taxation and tourism. The Interim Israeli-Palestinian Agreement of September 1995, constituting the third stage, broadened Palestinian self-government in the West Bank by means of an elected self-governing authority – the Palestinian Council – to allow the Palestinians to conduct their own internal affairs.

The last stage – negotiations between the parties on final status arrangements – began as scheduled in May 1996. These talks will determine the nature of the permanent settlement, covering remaining issues including refugees, settlements, security matters, borders, Jerusalem and other subjects of common interest.

Israel and Jordan: Three years of talks between Jordan and Israel following the Madrid Conference culminated in a declaration by King Hussein and Prime Minister Yitzhak Rabin (July 1994), which ended the 46-year state-of-war between their two countries. The Jordan-Israel peace treaty was signed at the Arava border crossing (near Eilat in Israel and Akaba in Jordan) on 26 October 1994, in the presence of American President Bill Clinton. Since then, Israel and Jordan have been cooperating in many spheres for the benefit of both countries.

Israel and Syria: Under the framework of the Madrid formula, talks between Israeli and Syrian delegations began in Washington and are held from time to time at ambassadorial level, with the involvement of high-ranking American officials. Two recent rounds of Syrian-Israeli peace talks (December 1995, January 1996), focused on security and other key issues. Highly detailed and comprehensive in scope, the talks identified important areas of conceptual agreement and convergence for future discussion and consideration.

Multilateral Talks

The multilateral talks were constituted as an integral part of the peace process, aimed at finding solutions for key regional problems, while serving as a confidence building measure to promote development of normalized relations among the Middle East nations. Following the Moscow Multilateral Middle East Conference (January 1992), with the participation of 36 countries and international organizations, the delegations broke up into five working groups dealing with specific areas of common regional concern – environment, arms control and regional security, refugees, water resources and economic development – which meet from time to time in various venues in the region.

The assassination of Prime Minister Yitzhak Rabin on 4 November 1995 by a Jewish extremist plunged the country into deep mourning for the soldier-statesman who had traveled from the battleground to lead the nation on the road to peace.

Israel Towards the 21st Century

After the assassination of Prime Minister Rabin (November 1995), the government – in accordance with its right to appoint a minister (who must also be a member of the Knesset) to serve as prime minister until the next elections – named Foreign Minister Shimon Peres as acting prime minister, with all the privileges of office except that of dissolving the Knesset. The May 1996 elections brought to power a coalition government made up of nationalist, religious and centrist elements, headed by Binyamin Netanyahu of the Likud.

With goals dedicated to the overall interests of the State of Israel, the challenges facing the new government are, *inter alia*, the continuation of the peace process; ensuring the country's security; broadening the scope of its diplomatic ties throughout the world; enhancing the education system by instituting smaller classes and a longer school day; promoting equal opportunity in education; placing increased emphasis on scientific and technological studies to assist Israeli industry; increasing economic competitiveness with less government intervention; reducing the balance-of-payments deficit; maintaining a low rate of inflation; streamlining government bureaucracy; easing the tax burden; finding solutions to housing problems; and intensifying infrastructure expansion. Steady immigration into the country and progress in the peace process should positively affect Israel's continued growth and development towards the coming century.

Peace unto this land

Archaeology in Israel has provided a valuable link between the country's past and present, with thousands of years of history unearthed at some 3,500 sites. Many finds attest to the long connection of the Jewish people with the Land of Israel, including Solomon's stables at Megiddo (Jezreel Valley), houses of the Israelite period in the City of David (Jerusalem), ritual baths at Masada, numerous synagogues and the Dead Sea scrolls, containing the earliest extant copy of the Book of Isaiah in still-legible Hebrew script. Excavations have also revealed vestiges of other civilizations which left their imprint on the Land over the centuries. All finds are recorded, and historical sites are carefully preserved and marked, for scholar and visitor alike.

HISTORICAL HIGHLIGHTS

(BCE – Before the Common Era)

17th–   **Biblical times**
6th C. BCE

c. 17th C.   Abraham, Isaac, Jacob – patriarchs of the Jewish people and bearers of a belief in One God – settle in the Land of Israel. Famine forces Israelites to migrate to Egypt

c. 13th C.   Moses leads Israelites from Egypt, followed by 40 years of wandering in the desert
Torah, including the Ten Commandments, received at Mount Sinai

13th–12th C.   Israelites settle in the Land of Israel

c. 1020   Jewish monarchy established; Saul, first king

c. 1000   Jerusalem made capital of David's kingdom

c. 960   First Temple, national and spiritual center of the Jewish people, built in Jerusalem by King Solomon

c. 930   Divided kingdom: Judah and Israel

722–720   Israel crushed by Assyrians; 10 tribes exiled (Ten Lost Tribes)

586   Judah conquered by Babylonia
Jerusalem and First Temple destroyed; most Jews exiled

538–142   **Persian and Hellenistic periods**

538–515   Many Jews return from Babylonia; Temple rebuilt

332   Land conquered by Alexander the Great; Hellenistic rule

166–160   Maccabean (Hasmonean) revolt against restrictions on practice of Judaism and desecration of the Temple

142–129   Jewish autonomy under Hasmoneans

129–63   Jewish independence under Hasmonean monarchy

63   Jerusalem captured by Roman general, Pompey

(CE – Common Era)

63 BCE– 313 CE	**Roman rule**
63–4 BCE	Herod, Roman vassal king, rules the Land of Israel Temple in Jerusalem refurbished
c. 20–33	Ministry of Jesus of Nazareth
66	Jewish revolt against Romans
70	Destruction of Jerusalem and Second Temple
73	Last stand of Jews at Masada
132–135	Bar Kokhba uprising against Rome
c. 210	Codification of Jewish oral law (*Mishnah*) completed
313–636	**Byzantine rule**
c. 390	Commentary on the Mishnah (Jerusalem *Talmud*) completed
614	Persian invasion
636–1099	**Arab rule**
691	On site of First and Second Temples in Jerusalem, Dome of the Rock built by Caliph Abd el-Malik
1099–1291	**Crusader domination (Latin Kingdom of Jerusalem)**
1291–1516	**Mamluk rule**
1517–1917	**Ottoman rule**
1564	Code of Jewish law (*Shulhan Arukh*) published
1860	First neighborhood built outside walls of Jerusalem
1882–1903	First Aliyah (large-scale immigration), mainly from Russia
1897	First Zionist Congress convened by Theodor Herzl in Basel, Switzerland; Zionist Organization founded
1904–14	Second Aliyah, mainly from Russia and Poland
1909	First kibbutz, Degania, and first modern all-Jewish city, Tel Aviv, founded
1917	400 years of Ottoman rule ended by British conquest British Foreign Minister Balfour pledges support for establishment of a "Jewish national home in Palestine"

1918–48	**British rule**
1919–23	Third Aliyah, mainly from Russia
1920	*Histadrut* (General Federation of Labor) and Haganah (Jewish defense organization) founded
	Vaad Leumi (National Council) set up by Jewish community (*yishuv*) to conduct its affairs
1921	First moshav, Nahalal, founded
1922	Britain granted Mandate for Palestine (Land of Israel) by League of Nations; Transjordan set up on three fourths of the area, leaving one fourth for the Jewish national home
	Jewish Agency representing Jewish community vis-a-vis Mandate authorities set up
1924	Technion, first institute of technology, founded in Haifa
1924–32	Fourth Aliyah, mainly from Poland
1925	Hebrew University of Jerusalem opened on Mt. Scopus
1929	Hebron Jews massacred by Arab militants
1931	*Etzel*, Jewish underground organization, founded
1933–39	Fifth Aliyah, mainly from Germany
1936–39	Anti-Jewish riots instigated by Arab militants
1939	Jewish immigration severely limited by British White Paper
1939–45	World War II: Holocaust in Europe
1940–41	*Lehi* underground movement formed; *Palmach*, strike force of Haganah, set up
1944	Jewish Brigade formed as part of British forces
1947	UN proposes establishment of Arab and Jewish states in the Land

1948	**State of Israel**
1948	End of British Mandate (14 May)
	State of Israel proclaimed (14 May)
	Israel invaded by five Arab states (15 May)
	Israel Defense Forces (IDF) formed
	War of Independence (May 1948–July 1949)

1949	Armistice agreements signed with Egypt, Jordan, Syria, Lebanon. Jerusalem divided under Israeli and Jordanian rule
	First *Knesset* (parliament) elected
	Israel admitted to United Nations as 59th member
1948–52	Mass immigration from Europe and Arab countries
1956	Sinai Campaign
1961–62	Adolf Eichmann tried and executed in Israel for his part in the Holocaust
1964	National Water Carrier completed, bringing water from Lake Kinneret in the north to the semi-arid south
1967	Six-Day War; Jerusalem reunited
1968–70	Egypt's War of Attrition against Israel
1973	Yom Kippur War
1975	Israel becomes an associate member of European Common Market
1977	Likud forms government after Knesset elections; end of 30 years of Labor rule
	Visit of Egyptian President Anwar Sadat to Jerusalem
1978	Camp David Accords include framework for comprehensive peace in the Middle East and proposal for Palestinian self-government
1979	Israel-Egypt Peace Treaty signed
	Prime Minister Menachem Begin and President Anwar Sadat awarded Nobel Peace Prize
1981	Israel Air Force destroys Iraqi nuclear reactor just before it is to become operative
1982	Israel's three-stage withdrawal from Sinai peninsula completed. Operation Peace for Galilee removes PLO (Palestine Liberation Organization) terrorists from Lebanon
1984	National unity government (Likud and Labor) formed after elections
	Operation Moses, immigration of Jews from Ethiopia
1985	Free Trade Agreement signed with United States
1987	Widespread violence (*intifada*) starts in Israeli-administered areas.

1988	Likud government in power following elections
1989	Four-point peace initiative proposed by Israel
	Start of mass immigration of Jews from former Soviet Union
1991	Israel attacked by Iraqi Scud missiles during Gulf War
	Middle East peace conference convened in Madrid
	Operation Solomon, airlift of Jews from Ethiopia
1992	Diplomatic relations established with China and India
	New government headed by Yitzhak Rabin of Labor party
1993	Declaration of Principles on Interim Self-Government Arrangements for the Palestinians signed by Israel and PLO, as representative of the Palestinian people
1994	Implementation of Palestinian self-government in Gaza Strip and Jericho area
	Full diplomatic relations with the Holy See
	Morocco and Tunisia interest offices set up
	Israel-Jordan Peace Treaty signed
	Rabin, Peres, Arafat awarded Nobel Peace Prize
1995	Broadened Palestinian self-government implemented in West Bank and Gaza Strip; Palestinian Council elected
	Prime Minister Yitzhak Rabin assassinated at peace rally
	Shimon Peres becomes prime minister
1996	Fundamentalist Arab terrorism against Israel escalates
	Operation Grapes of Wrath, retaliation for Hizbullah terrorists' attacks on northern Israel
	Trade representation offices set up in Oman and Qatar
	Likud forms government after Knesset elections
	Omani trade representation office opened in Tel Aviv

the state

The State

Political Structure

The Presidency

Legislature: The Knesset

Executive: The Government

The Judiciary

Local Government

Israel Defense Forces (IDF)

...ותשועה ברב יועץ.
(משלי י״א: י״ד)

...in the multitude of counselors
there is safety.
(Proverbs 11:14)

The Declaration of the Establishment of the State of Israel, signed on 14 May 1948 by members of the National Council representing the Jewish community in the country and the Zionist movement abroad, constitutes the nation's credo. Included therein are the historical imperatives of Israel's rebirth; the framework for a democratic Jewish state founded on liberty, justice and peace, as envisaged by the biblical prophets; and a call for peaceful relations with the neighboring Arab states for the benefit of the entire region.

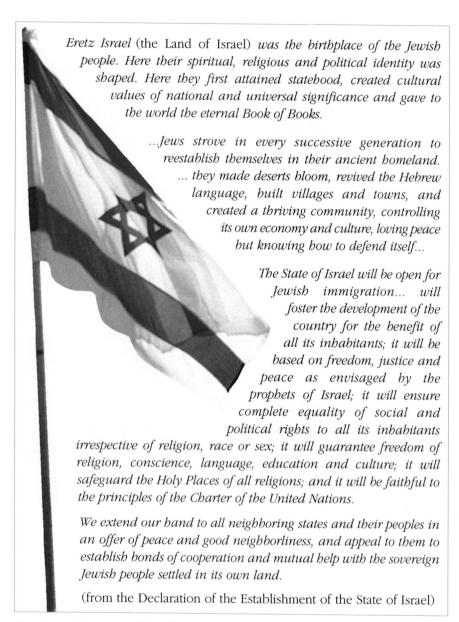

Eretz Israel (the Land of Israel) *was the birthplace of the Jewish people. Here their spiritual, religious and political identity was shaped. Here they first attained statehood, created cultural values of national and universal significance and gave to the world the eternal Book of Books.*

...Jews strove in every successive generation to reestablish themselves in their ancient homeland. ... they made deserts bloom, revived the Hebrew language, built villages and towns, and created a thriving community, controlling its own economy and culture, loving peace but knowing how to defend itself...

The State of Israel will be open for Jewish immigration... will foster the development of the country for the benefit of all its inhabitants; it will be based on freedom, justice and peace as envisaged by the prophets of Israel; it will ensure complete equality of social and political rights to all its inhabitants irrespective of religion, race or sex; it will guarantee freedom of religion, conscience, language, education and culture; it will safeguard the Holy Places of all religions; and it will be faithful to the principles of the Charter of the United Nations.

We extend our hand to all neighboring states and their peoples in an offer of peace and good neighborliness, and appeal to them to establish bonds of cooperation and mutual help with the sovereign Jewish people settled in its own land.

(from the Declaration of the Establishment of the State of Israel)

The flag of the State of Israel is based on the design of the Jewish prayer shawl (*tallit*), with a blue Shield of David (*Magen David*)

The official emblem of the State of Israel is a candelabra (*menorah*), whose shape is said to be derived from the seven-branched *moriah*, a plant known since antiquity. The olive branches on either side represent Israel's yearning for peace.

HATIKVAH – THE NATIONAL ANTHEM

Kol od ba-le-vav pe-ni - mah

ne - fesh ye - hu - di ho - mi - yah, U - le

fa - a - tey miz - rah ka - di - mah

a - yin le - Tzi - yon tzo - fi - yah,

Od lo av' - dah tik - va - te - nu,

Ha - tik - vah bat sh'not al - pa - yim,

Li - h'yot am hof - shi be - ar - tze - nu,

E - retz Tzi - yon vi - ru - sha - la - yim.

Li - h'yot am hof - shi be - ar - tze - nu,

E - retz Tzi - yon vi - ru - sha - la - yim.

כָּל עוֹד בַּלֵּבָב פְּנִימָה
נֶפֶשׁ יְהוּדִי הוֹמִיָּה
וּלְפַאֲתֵי מִזְרָח קָדִימָה
עַיִן לְצִיּוֹן צוֹפִיָּה
עוֹד לֹא אָבְדָה תִּקְוָתֵנוּ
הַתִּקְוָה בַּת שְׁנוֹת אַלְפַּיִם
לִהְיוֹת עַם חָפְשִׁי בְּאַרְצֵנוּ
אֶרֶץ צִיּוֹן וִירוּשָׁלַיִם.

As long as deep in the heart,
The soul of a Jew yearns,
And towards the East,
An eye looks to Zion,
Our hope is not yet lost,
The hope of two thousand years,
To be a free people in our land,
The land of Zion and Jerusalem.

POLITICAL STRUCTURE

Israel is a parliamentary democracy consisting of legislative, executive and judicial branches. Its institutions are the presidency, the *Knesset* (parliament), the government (cabinet of ministers) and the judiciary. The system is based on the principle of separation of powers, with checks and balances, in which the executive branch (the government) is subject to the confidence of the legislative branch (the Knesset) and the independence of the judiciary is guaranteed by law.

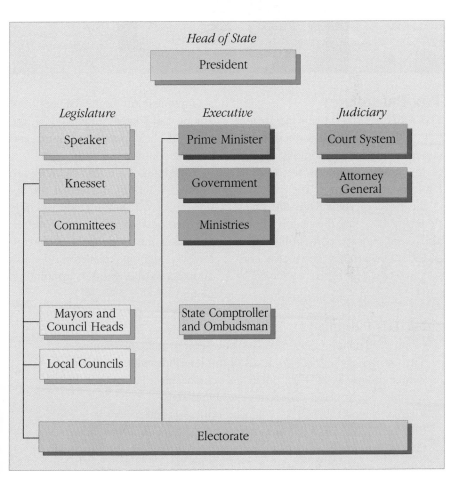

THE PRESIDENCY

The *nasi* (president) bears the ancient title of the head of the Sanhedrin, the supreme legislative and judicial body of the Jewish people in the Land of Israel in ancient times. The president is the head of state, with the presidency symbolizing the nation's unity, above and beyond party politics. The president, who may serve two consecutive five-year terms, is elected by a simple majority of the Knesset from among candidates nominated on the basis of their personal stature and lifelong contribution to the state.

Presidential duties, which are mostly ceremonial and formal, are defined by law. They include opening the first session of a new Knesset; accepting the credentials of foreign envoys; signing treaties and laws adopted by the Knesset; appointing,

---

ISRAEL'S PRESIDENTS

Chaim Weizmann (1949–52), Zionist leader, prominent scientist
Yitzhak Ben-Zvi (1952–63), head of the Jewish Agency, historian
Zalman Shazar (1963–73), politician, scholar, historian, author, poet
Ephraim Katzir (1973–78), renowned biochemist
Yitzhak Navon (1978–83), politician, educator, author
Chaim Herzog (1983–93), attorney, army general, diplomat, author
Ezer Weizman (1993–   ), air force general, politician, businessman

---

on recommendation of appropriate bodies, the heads of Israel's diplomatic missions abroad, judges and the governor of the Bank of Israel; and pardoning prisoners, on advice of the minister of justice. In addition, the president performs public functions and informal tasks such as hearing citizens' appeals, lending prestige to community organizations and strengthening campaigns to improve the quality of life in the society at large.

LEGISLATURE: THE KNESSET

The Knesset (Israel's unicameral parliament) is the country's legislative body. The Knesset took its name and fixed its membership at 120 from the *Knesset Hagedolah* (Great Assembly), the representative Jewish council convened in Jerusalem by Ezra and Nehemiah in the 5th century BCE.

A new Knesset begins to function after general elections, which determine its composition. In the first session, Knesset members declare their allegiance, and the Knesset speaker and deputy speakers are elected. The Knesset usually serves for four years, but may dissolve itself or be dissolved by the prime minister any time during its term. Until a new Knesset is formally constituted following elections, full authority remains with the outgoing one.

The Knesset operates in plenary sessions and through 12 standing committees: the House Committee; the Foreign Affairs and Security Committee; the Finance Committee; the Interior and Environment Committee; the Education and Culture Committee; the Labor and Welfare Committee; the Constitution, Law and Justice Committee; the Immigration and Absorption Committee; the State Control Committee; the Committee against Drug Abuse; and the Committee for Advancing the Status of Women.

In plenary sessions, general debates are conducted on legislation submitted by the government or by individual Knesset members, as well as on government policy and activity. Debates are conducted in Hebrew, but members may speak Arabic, as both are official languages. Simultaneous translation is available.

To become law, a bill must pass three readings in the Knesset. In the first reading, the bill is presented to the plenary, followed by a short debate on its contents, after which it is referred to the appropriate Knesset committee for detailed discussion and redrafting, if necessary. When the committee has completed its work, the bill is returned to the plenary for its second reading, at which time committee members who have reservations may present them to the plenary. Following a general debate, each article of the bill is put to a vote and, unless it is necessary to return it again to committee, the third reading takes place immediately, and a vote is taken on the bill as a whole.

If the bill passes, it is signed by the presiding speaker and is later published in the Official Gazette, with the signatures of the president, prime minister, Knesset speaker and the minister responsible for the law's implementation. Finally, the state seal is placed on it by the minister of justice, and the bill becomes law.

EXECUTIVE: THE GOVERNMENT

The executive authority of the state is the government (cabinet of ministers), charged with administering internal and foreign affairs, including security matters. Its policy-making powers are very wide, and it is authorized to take action on any issue which is not delegated by law to another authority.

The government determines its own working and decision-making procedures. It usually meets once a week, but additional meetings may be called as needed. It may also act through ministerial committees.

All governments to date have been based on coalitions of several parties, since no party has ever received enough Knesset seats to form a government by itself.

To form a government, the newly-elected prime minister has to present, within 45 days of publication of the election results, a list of ministers for Knesset approval, together with an outline of proposed government guidelines.

Once approved, the ministers are responsible to the prime minister for the fulfillment of their duties and accountable to the Knesset for their actions. Most ministers are assigned a portfolio and head a ministry; ministers who function without portfolio may be called upon to assume responsibility for special projects. The prime minister may serve also as a minister with a portfolio.

The number of ministers, including the prime minister, may not exceed 18 nor be less than eight. At least half must be Knesset members, but all must be eligible for Knesset membership. The prime minister, or another minister with prime ministerial approval, may appoint deputy ministers, up to a total of six; all must be Knesset members.

Like the Knesset, the government usually serves for four years, but its term may be shortened by the resignation or death of the prime minister, or a vote of no-confidence by the Knesset. The prime minister and ministers of an outgoing government continue their duties until a new prime minister and a new government begin their term.

If the prime minister is unable to continue in office due to death, resignation, impeachment or a Knesset vote of no-confidence, the government appoints one of its members (who must also be a Knesset member) as acting prime minister; he assumes all the powers of office except the authority to dissolve the Knesset. Other ministers continue to fulfill their duties until a new prime minister is elected and takes office.

ELECTIONS

Elections for the Knesset and the prime minister are held at the same time. The entire country constitutes a single electoral constituency, and all citizens are eligible to vote from age 18. On election day, voters cast two secret ballots, one for the prime minister and another for a political party to represent them in the Knesset.

Election day is a national holiday, free transportation is available to voters who happen to be outside their polling district on that day and polling stations are provided for military personnel, hospital patients and prisoners, as well as for merchant seamen and Israelis on assignment abroad. A central elections committee, headed by a justice of the Supreme Court and including representatives of the parties holding Knesset seats, is responsible for conducting the elections. Regional election committees oversee the proper functioning of local polling committees, which include representatives of at least three parties in the outgoing Knesset. In each election to date, between 77 and 90 percent of all registered voters have cast their ballots, expressing the great interest taken by most Israelis in their national and local politics.

Knesset elections are based on a vote for a party rather than for individuals, and the many political parties which run for the Knesset reflect a wide range of outlooks and beliefs.

The two main parties – Labor, essentially social-democratic, and Likud, substantially national-liberal – have historical roots and traditions pre-dating the establishment of the state in 1948, and both began to crystallize into their present form in 1965. In recent years they have become increasingly populist and relatively pragmatic, compared to the parties to their left and right. Neither party has ever attained a majority of Knesset seats. For decades, Labor and Likud have together held about two thirds of the Knesset membership, with the remaining seats gained by small parties, which may be roughly divided into several groupings: national-religious, ultra-orthodox religious, centrist, left-wing, nationalist, immigrants' and Arab parties. However, in the 1996 elections, the two large parties together received just over half of the seats, with the small parties increasing in strength.

Prior to elections, each party presents its platform and a list of Knesset candidates in order of precedence, determined through various internal

procedures; candidates must be Israeli citizens over 21 years of age. The president, state comptroller, judges and senior public officials, as well as the chief-of-staff and high-ranking military officers, are disqualified from presenting their candidacy unless they have resigned their position at least 100 days before the elections.

Parties in the outgoing Knesset automatically stand for reelection; other parties may present their candidacy by obtaining the signatures of 2,500 eligible voters and depositing a bond, which is refunded if they succeed in receiving at least 1.5 percent of the national vote, entitling them to one Knesset seat. Knesset seats are assigned in proportion to each party's percentage of the total national vote. A party's surplus votes, insufficient for an additional seat, are redistributed among the various parties according to their proportional size, or as agreed between parties prior to the elections. A treasury allocation for election campaigns is granted to each party based on its number of seats in the outgoing Knesset. New parties receive a similar allocation retroactively for each member elected. The state comptroller reviews the disbursement of all campaign expenditures.

Candidates for prime minister may be nominated by a party, or parties, with at least 10 seats in the outgoing Knesset, or by 50,000 enfranchised persons. Candidates must be Israeli citizens, over 30 years old and heading a party running for the Knesset. A prime minister who has served for seven consecutive years is not eligible for reelection.

In the elections, the candidate who receives over half of the valid votes becomes the prime minister. In the event that no candidate receives more than half, run-off elections are held two weeks later between the two candidates with the most votes. Should a candidate die or be unable to participate in the run-off elections for health reasons, the name of another candidate may be submitted by the same nominating body no later than 96 hours before the scheduled elections. If one of the run-off candidates resigns, the nominee with the next largest number of valid votes becomes the replacement candidate. When only one candidate runs, either in the general or run-off elections, the vote is taken for or against candidacy. Should the number of valid votes in favor of the candidate be higher than those opposed, the candidate is elected. In the event of a tie, new elections for the prime minister are held.

The prime minister's term of office corresponds to that of the Knesset (four years) except if it is cut short for one reason or another. Whether the elections that follow will be held for the prime minister only (special elections), or for the Knesset as well, is specified by law.

ISRAEL'S PRIME MINISTERS

David Ben-Gurion (1948–54)

Moshe Sharett (1954–55)

David Ben-Gurion (1955–63)

Levi Eshkol (1963–69)

Golda Meir (1969–74)

Yitzhak Rabin (1974–77)

Menachem Begin (1977–83)

Yitzhak Shamir (1983–84)

Shimon Peres (1984–86)

Yitzhak Shamir (1986–92)

Yitzhak Rabin (1992–95)

Shimon Peres (1995–96)

Binyamin Netanyahu (1996–)

The Judiciary

The independence of the judiciary is guaranteed by law. Judges are appointed by the president, upon recommendation of a nominations committee comprised of Supreme Court judges, members of the bar and public figures. Appointments are permanent, with mandatory retirement at age 70.

The Court System

Magistrates' Court (1 judge)	Civil and minor criminal offenses; jurisdiction in civil and criminal cases.
District Court (1 or 3 judges)	Appellate jurisdiction over magistrates' courts; original jurisdiction in more important civil and criminal cases.
Supreme Court (1, 3, 5 or a larger uneven number of judges)	Ultimate appellate jurisdiction nationwide; right to address issues when necessary to intervene for the sake of justice; authority to release persons illegally detained or imprisoned; sitting as a High Court of Justice, hears petitions against any government body or agent and is the court of first and last instance.
Special Courts (1 judge)	Traffic, labor, juvenile, military and municipal courts, with clearly defined jurisdiction; administrative tribunals.
Religious Courts (1 or 3 judges)	Jurisdiction in matters of personal status (marriage, divorce, maintenance, guardianship, adoption) vested in judicial institutions of respective religious communities: Jewish rabbinical courts, Muslim *sharia* courts, Druze religious courts, ecclesiastical courts of the ten recognized Christian communities in Israel.

LAW OF THE LAND

Upon attaining independence (1948), Israel passed the Law and Administration Ordinance, stipulating that laws prevailing in the country prior to statehood would remain in force insofar as they did not contradict the principles embodied in the Declaration of the Establishment of the State of Israel or would not conflict with laws to be enacted by the Knesset. Thus the legal system includes remnants of Ottoman law (in force until 1917), British Mandate laws, which incorporate a large body of English common law, elements of Jewish religious law and some aspects of other systems. However, the prevailing characteristic of the legal system is the large corpus of independent statutory and case law which has been evolving since 1948.

Following the establishment of the state, the Knesset was empowered to enact a series of basic laws, relating to all aspects of life, which would eventually be brought together to form a constitution. Most chapters have already been passed as Basic Laws outlining the fundamental features of government such as the President, the Knesset, the Government, the Judicature, Israel Defense Forces, the State Comptroller, Freedom of Occupation (dealing with the right to follow the vocation of one's choosing)

and Human Dignity and Liberty, which addresses protections against violation of a person's life, body or dignity. The normative superiority of Basic Laws over ordinary legislation was confirmed in 1995, when the Supreme Court assumed the power of judicial review of Knesset legislation violating a Basic Law.

Over the years, a body of case law has developed through Supreme Court rulings which protect civil liberties, including freedom of speech, freedom of assembly, freedom of religion, and equality as fundamental values of Israel's legal system. In its capacity as a High Court of Justice and acting as the court of first and last instance, the Supreme Court also hears petitions brought by individuals appealing for redress against any government body or agent.

ATTORNEY GENERAL

The government's legal service is headed by the attorney-general, who holds exclusive power to represent the state in all major criminal, civil and administrative matters. The government is bound to abstain from any action which, in the opinion of the attorney-general, is unlawful, as long as the courts do not rule otherwise. Although appointed by the government, the attorney-general functions independently of the political system.

ISRAEL POLICE

In common with police forces around the world, the task of Israel's police is to maintain the quality of life by fighting crime, assisting the authorities in carrying out the law and enforcing traffic regulations, as well as providing guidance on preventive measures for the safety and protection of the population.

The police's principal mobile task force, the Border Guard, deals mainly with internal security problems and includes a special anti-terrorist unit. The frequency and threat of terrorist incidents led concerned citizens to request active participation in the protection of their communities. Thus, a volunteer civil guard was established (1974) to maintain neighborhood security units, including command centers, armed patrols and training programs.

PRISON SERVICE

Separate prison facilities are maintained for adult male criminals, security prisoners, white-collar offenders, juveniles and women. A variety of rehabilitation programs are available, geared to the inmates' profile and offense and aimed at their reintegration into society. Among them are educational and vocational courses; probation frameworks; counseling; and employment opportunities within and outside prison, with earnings divided equally among prisoners, their families and savings schemes. Home leave is granted every 2-3 months to all prisoners except those considered a danger to public safety.

The right of the prisoner to early release is provided by law. Inmates sentenced to more than six months may be discharged at the discretion of the Release Committee after having served two thirds of their sentence. Prisoners serving a life sentence may appeal to the president for either a pardon or a reduction of sentence. The Ministry of Labor and Social Affairs, assisted by volunteer organizations, contributes to the rehabilitation of prisoners by working with their families and, upon their release, supporting their efforts to secure employment and maintain a normative lifestyle.

The State Comptroller, established by law (1949) to assure public accountability, the state comptroller carries out external audit and reports on the legality, regularity, economy, efficiency, effectiveness and moral integrity of public administration. Since 1971, the state comptroller also serves as ombudsman, receiving complaints from the public against state or public bodies subject to the comptroller's audit. The state comptroller is elected by the Knesset in a secret ballot for a five-year term and is responsible only to the Knesset. The comptroller has unrestricted access to the accounts, files and personnel of all bodies subject to audit. The scope of state audit includes the activities of all government ministries, state institutions, branches of the defense establishment, local authorities, government corporations, state enterprises and others. In addition, the state comptroller is empowered by law to inspect the financial affairs of the political parties represented in the Knesset as well as their election campaign accounts, imposing monetary sanctions when irregularities are found.

LOCAL GOVERNMENT

Services provided by local government include education, culture, health, social welfare, road maintenance, public parks, water and sanitation. Each local authority functions through by-laws, complementing national laws, which have been approved by the Ministry of the Interior. Some authorities operate special courts in which transgressors of local by-laws are tried. Financing for local authorities comes from local taxes as well as allocations from the state budget. Every authority has a comptroller who prepares an annual report.

The law recognizes three types of local authorities: municipalities which provide the framework for urban centers with populations of over 20,000; local councils which manage towns with populations of between 2,000 and 20,000; and regional councils which are responsible for several villages grouped within a certain radius. Each local authority is administered by a mayor or chairperson and a council. The number of council members is determined by the Ministry of the Interior, according to the authority's population. Currently there are 57 municipalities, 145 local councils and 55 regional councils.

All municipalities and local councils are united, on a voluntary basis, in a central body, the Union of Local Authorities, which represents them before the government, monitors relevant legislation in the Knesset and provides guidance on issues such as work agreements and legal affairs. Affiliated with the International Association of Municipalities, the Union maintains ties with like organizations throughout the world, arranges twin cities programs and exchanges of international delegations.

In regional council elections, one candidate in each village is elected by simple plurality, with those elected becoming members of the council. Heads of regional councils are selected from among the regional council's members.

Local elections are financed by government appropriations, on the basis of the number of mandates that each faction or list wins in the local authority.

LOCAL ELECTIONS

Elections for local government are conducted by secret ballot every five years. All permanent residents, whether Israeli citizens or not, whose names appear on the voter registry of a particular authority are eligible to vote in local elections from age 18 and to be elected from age 21.

In elections for municipal and local councils, ballots are cast for a party list of candidates, with the number of council seats attained by each list proportional to the percentage of votes received. Mayors and chairpersons of local councils are elected directly.

ISRAEL DEFENSE FORCES (IDF)

The IDF, founded in 1948, ranks among the most battle-trained armed forces in the world, having had to defend the country in five major wars. Currently, the IDF's security objectives are to defend the existence, territorial integrity and sovereignty of the State of Israel, deter all enemies and curb all forms of terrorism which threaten daily life. Its main tasks include reinforcing the peace arrangements; ensuring overall security in the West Bank and Gaza Strip in coordination with the Palestinian Authority; spearheading the war against terrorism, both inside Israel and across its borders; and maintaining a deterrent capability to prevent the outbreak of hostilities.

To ensure its success, the IDF's doctrine at the strategic level is defensive, while its tactics are offensive. Given the country's lack of territorial depth, the IDF must take initiative when deemed necessary and, if attacked, to quickly transfer the battleground to the enemy's land. Though it has always been outnumbered by its enemies, the IDF maintains a qualitative advantage by deploying advanced weapons systems, many of which are developed and manufactured in Israel for its specific needs. The IDF's main resource, however, is the high calibre of its soldiers.

In preparing for defense, the IDF deploys a small standing army (made up of conscripts and career personnel) with early warning capability, and a regular air force and navy. The majority of its forces are reservists, who are called up regularly for training and service and who, in time of war or crisis, are quickly mobilized into their units from all parts of the country.

The IDF's three service branches (ground forces, air force and navy) function under a unified command, headed by the chief-of-staff, with the rank of lieutenant-general, who is responsible to the Minister of Defense. The chief-of staff is appointed by the government, on recommendation of the prime minister and minister of defense, for a three-year term, which is usually extended for an additional year.

Except when combat duty is involved, men and women soldiers of all ranks serve side by side as technicians, communications and intelligence specialists, combat instructors, cartographers, administrative and ordnance personnel, computer operators, doctors, lawyers and the like.

The IDF is responsive to the cultural and social needs of its soldiers, providing recreational and educational activities, as well as personal support services. Recruits with incomplete educational backgrounds are given opportunities to upgrade their level of education, and career officers are encouraged to study at the IDF's expense during their service. The integration of new immigrant soldiers is facilitated through special Hebrew language instruction and other programs. Active in nation-building enterprises since its inception, the IDF also provides remedial and supplementary education to civilian populations and contributes to the absorption of newcomers among the population at large. In times of national crisis or emergency, the IDF responds immediately with appropriate action and assigns trained personnel to fill essential jobs or carry out special tasks.

TERMS OF SERVICE IN THE IDF

Compulsory Service: All eligible men and women are drafted at age 18. Men serve for three years, women for 21 months. Deferments may be granted to qualified students at institutions of higher education. New immigrants may be deferred or serve for shorter periods of time, depending on their age and personal status on entering the country.

Reserve Duty: Upon completion of compulsory service, each soldier is assigned to a reserve unit. Men up to age 51 serve up to 39 days a year, a period of time which can be extended in times of emergency. Recent policy has been to reduce the burden of reserve duty whenever possible, and reservists who have served in combat units may now be discharged at age 45.

Career Military Service: Veterans of compulsory service meeting current IDF needs may sign up as career officers or NCOs. The career service constitutes the command and administrative backbone of the IDF. Graduates of officers' or pilots' schools or special military technical schools are required to sign on for periods of career service.

LAND AND PEOPLE

THE LAND

NATURE

INFRASTRUCTURE

URBAN LIFE

RURAL LIFE

...ארץ זבת חלב ודבש ...

(שמות ג': ח')

...a land flowing with milk and honey ...

(Exodus 3:8)

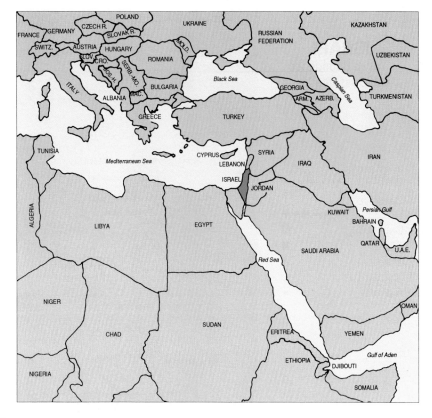

Israel is a small, narrow, semi-arid country on the southeastern coastline of the Mediterranean Sea. It entered history some 35 centuries ago when the Jewish people forsook their nomadic way of life, settled in the Land and became a nation. Over the years, the Land was known by many names – Eretz Israel (Land of Israel); Zion, one of Jerusalem's hills which came to signify both the city and the Land of Israel as a whole; Palestine, derived from Philistia, and first used by the Romans; the Promised Land; and the Holy Land, to mention but a few. However, to most Israelis today, the country is simply Ha'aretz – the Land. Over 5.5 million people live in Israel today. Some 4.5 million are Jews; most of the remaining million are Arabs. A wide spectrum of lifestyles characterize the country, ranging from religious to secular, from modern to traditional, from urban to rural, from communal to individual.

ISRAEL
Within Boundaries
and Ceasefire Lines

LEGEND

International Boundary — · — · —

Ceasefire Line — — — — —

Capital City ✪

City ■

Town ☐

Palestinian Authority ●

MEDITERRANEAN SEA

LEBANON

SYRIA

GOLAN

Kiryat Shemona
Katzrin
Safad
Nahariya
Akko
GALILEE
Tiberias
LAKE KINNERET
Haifa
Nazareth
Afula
Beit She'an
Hadera
Jenin
Tulkarm
Netanya
SAMARIA
Kalkilye
Nablus
Ramat Gan
Bnei Brak
Ariel
Tel Aviv - Yafo
Petah Tikva
Bat Yam
Holon
Rishon Lezion
Ramla
Ramallah
Rehovot
Jericho
Ashdod
Jerusalem
Beit Shemesh
Bethlehem
Ashkelon
DEAD SEA
Gaza
Hebron
Netivot
JUDEA
Arad
Be'er Sheva
JORDAN
Jordan River
Dimona
Yeroham
NEGEV
EGYPT
Eilat

Scale: 1 : 2,300,000

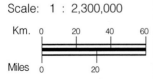

Km. 0   20   40   60

Miles 0   20

Copyright © Atir Ltd. Rehovot, Israel

THE LAND

SMALL AREA; SHORT DISTANCES

Israel's area within boundaries and cease-fire lines, including the areas under Palestinian self-government, is 10,840 square miles (27,800 sq.km.). Long and narrow in shape, it is some 290 miles (470 km.) in length and about 85 miles (135 km.) across at the widest point. The country is bordered by Lebanon to the north, Syria to the northeast, Jordan to the east, Egypt to the southwest and the Mediterranean Sea to the west.

Mountains and plains, fertile fields and desert are often minutes apart. The width of the country, from the Mediterranean Sea in the west to the Dead Sea in the east, can be crossed by car in about 90 minutes; and the trip from Metulla, in the far north, to Eilat at the country's southern tip takes about nine hours.

GEOGRAPHICAL FEATURES

Israel may be divided into four geographical regions: three parallel strips running north to south and a large, mostly arid zone in the southern half.

The **coastal plain** runs parallel to the Mediterranean Sea and is composed of a sandy shoreline, bordered by stretches of fertile farmland extending up to 25 miles (40 km.) inland. In the north, expanses of sandy beach are occasionally punctuated by jagged chalk and sandstone cliffs. The coastal plain is home to more than half of Israel's over 5.5 million people and includes major urban centers, deep-water harbors, most of the country's industry and a large part of its agriculture and tourist facilities.

Several **mountain ranges** run the length of the country. In the northeast, the basalt landscapes of the Golan Heights, formed by volcanic eruptions in the distant past, rise as steep cliffs overlooking the Hula Valley. The hills of Galilee, largely composed of soft limestone and dolomite, ascent to heights ranging from 1,600 to 4,000 feet (500 to 1,200 m.) above sea level. Small perennial streams and relatively ample rainfall keep the area green all year round. Residents of Galilee and the Golan, some 17 percent of the population, are engaged in agriculture, tourism-related enterprises and light industry.

The Jezreel Valley, separating the hills of Galilee from those of Samaria, is Israel's richest agricultural area, cultivated by many cooperative communities (kibbutzim and moshavim). The rolling hills of Samaria and Judea present a mosaic of rocky hilltops and fertile valleys, dotted with groves of age-old, silver-green olive trees. The terraced hillsides, first developed by farmers in ancient times, blend into the natural landscape. The population is concentrated mainly in small urban centers and large villages.

The **Negev**, comprising about half of Israel's land area, is inhabited by only 8 percent of the population, living mainly in the northern part, supported by an agricultural and industrial economy. Further south, the Negev becomes an arid zone characterized by low sandstone hills and plains, abounding with canyons and wadis in which winter rains often produce flash floods. Continuing southward, the region gives way to an area of bare craggy peaks, craters and rock-strewn plateaus, where the climate is drier and the mountains are higher. Three erosive craters, the largest of which is about 5 miles (8 km.) across and 21 miles (35 km.) long, cut deeply into the earth's crust, displaying a broad range of colors and rock types. At the tip of the Negev, near Eilat on the Red Sea, sharp pinnacles of gray and red granite are broken by dry gorges and sheer cliffs, with colorful layers of sandstone glowing in the sunlight.

streams from Mount Hermon, it runs through the fertile Hula Valley into Lake Kinneret (Sea of Galilee) and continues winding through the Jordan Valley before emptying into the Dead Sea. While it swells during the winter rainy season, the river is usually quite narrow and shallow.

Lake Kinneret, nestled between the hills of Galilee and the Golan Heights at 695 feet (212 m.) below sea level, is 5 miles (8 km.) wide and 13 miles (21 km.) long. It is Israel's largest lake and serves as the country's main water reservoir. Along the Kinneret's shores are some important historical and religious sites, as well as agricultural communities, fishing enterprises and tourist facilities.

The **Jordan Valley** and the Arava, running the length of the country in the east, are part of the Syrian-African Rift which split the earth's crust millions of years ago. Its northern stretches are extremely fertile, while the southern portion is semi-arid. Agriculture, fishing, light industry and tourism constitute the area's main sources of income. The Jordan River, flowing from north to south through the Rift, descends over 2,300 feet (700 m.) in the course of its 186 mile (300 km.) route. Fed by

The Arava, Israel's savannah region, begins south of the Dead Sea and extends to the Gulf of Eilat, Israel's outlet to the Red Sea. Adaptation of sophisticated farming techniques to climatic conditions, where the average annual rainfall is less than one inch (25 mm.) and summer temperatures soar to 104°F (40° C), has made it possible to grow out-of-season fruit and vegetables, mainly for export. The sub-tropical Gulf of Eilat, noted for its deep blue waters, coral reefs and exotic marine life, lies at the southern tip of the Arava.

The **Dead Sea**, the lowest point on earth at about 1,300 feet (400 m.) below sea level, lies at the southern end of the Jordan Valley. Its waters, with the highest level of salinity and density in the world, are rich in potash, magnesium and bromine, as well as in table and industrial salts. The Dead Sea's natural pace of recession has been accelerated in recent years due to a very high rate of evaporation (5 feet–1.6 m. annually) and large-scale diversion projects undertaken by Israel and Jordan for their water needs, causing a 75 percent reduction in the incoming flow of water. As a result, the surface level of the Dead Sea has dropped some 35 feet (10.6 m.) since 1960. A project to link the Dead Sea with the Mediterranean Sea by means of a canal and pipe system, which may help restore the Dead Sea to its natural dimensions and level, is under consideration.

CLIMATE

Israel's climate ranges from temperate to tropical, with plenty of sunshine. Two distinct seasons predominate: a rainy winter period from November to May; and a dry summer season which extends through the next six months. Rainfall is relatively heavy in the north and center of the country, with much less in the northern Negev and almost negligible amounts in the southern areas. Regional conditions vary considerably, with humid summers and mild winters on the coast; dry summers and moderately cold winters in the hill regions, hot dry summers and pleasant winters in the Jordan Valley; and year-round semi-desert conditions in the Negev. Weather extremes range from occasional winter snowfall at higher elevations to periodic oppressively hot dry winds which send temperatures soaring, particularly in spring and autumn.

Temperatures (minimum-maximum)								
		Safed	Haifa	Tiberias	Tel Aviv	Jerusalem	Be'er Sheva	Eilat
January	F°	31-48	48-59	45-64	48-63	43-52	43-61	48-70
	C°	4-9	9-15	8-18	9-17	6-11	6-16	9-21
August	F°	64-84	72-82	72-97	72-84	66-82	66-91	77-104
	C°	18-29	22-28	22-36	22-29	19-28	19-33	25-39

Rainfall (average)								
		Safed	Haifa	Tiberias	Tel Aviv	Jerusalem	Be'er Sheva	Eilat
Number of days		75	66	57	64	57	33	8
Mean annual rainfall	inches	28	20	17	22	19	8	1
	mm.	718	508	431	539	486	204	25

WATER

Located on the edge of a desert belt, Israel has always suffered a scarcity of water. Archaeological discoveries in the Negev and other parts of the country reveal that local inhabitants thousands of years ago were already concerned with water conservation, as evidenced by a variety of systems, designed to both collect and store rainwater and transfer it from one place to another. The total annual renewable water resources amount to some 60 billion cubic feet (1.7 billion cu.m.), of which about 75 percent is used for irrigation and the balance for urban and industrial purposes. The country's water sources consist of the Jordan River, Lake Kinneret and a few small river systems. Natural springs and underground water tables, tapped in controlled quantities to prevent depletion and salination, are also utilized. As maximum use has been made of all freshwater sources, ways are being developed to exploit marginal water resources through the recycling of waste water, cloud-seeding and desalination of brackish water.

To overcome regional imbalances in water availability, most of Israel's freshwater sources are joined in an integrated grid. Its central artery, the National Water Carrier, completed in 1964, brings water from the north and central regions, through a network of giant pipes, aqueducts, open canals, reservoirs, tunnels, dams and pumping stations, to the semi-arid south.

NATURE

FLORA AND FAUNA

Israel's plant and animal life is rich and diversified, in part due to the country's geographical location at the junction of three continents. Over 2,800 types of plants have been identified, ranging from alpine species on the northern mountain slopes to Saharan species in the Arava in the south. Israel is the northernmost limit for the presence of plants such as the papyrus reed and the southernmost limit for others like the bright red coral peony.

Natural woodlands, consisting mostly of calliprinos oaks, cover parts of Galilee, Mount Carmel and other hilly areas. In spring, the rockrose and throny broom predominate with a color scheme of pink, white and yellow. Honeysuckle creeps over the bushes, and large plane trees provide

shade along the freshwater streams of Galilee. In the Negev highlands, massive Atlantic pistachios strike a dramatic note along the dry valleys, and date palms grow wherever there is sufficient underground water.

Many cultivated flowers such as the iris, madonna lily, tulip and hyacinth have relatives among the wild flowers of Israel. Soon after the first rains in October-November, the country is covered by a green carpet which lasts until the return of the summer dry season. Pink and white cyclamen and red, white and purple anemones bloom from December to March, with the blue lupin and yellow corn marigold flowering a little later. Many native plants such as the crocus and squill are geophytes, which store nourishment in bulbs or tubers and bloom at the end of the summer. Hovering over the fields are some 135 varieties of butterflies of brilliant hues and patterns.

Over 380 different species of birds can be seen in Israel. Some, like the common bulbul, are resident in the country; others such as coots and starlings spend the winter feasting on food provided by Israel's fishponds and farmland. Hundreds of thousands of birds migrate twice yearly along the length of the country, providing magnificent opportunities for bird-watching. Honey buzzards, pelicans

and other large and small migrants fill the skies in March and October. Several raptor species, among them eagles, falcons and hawks, and tiny songbirds such as sylvia warblers and goldcrests nest in Israel.

Delicate mountain gazelles roam over the hills; foxes, jungle cats and other mammals live in wooded areas; Nubian ibex with majestic horns leap over desert crags; and chameleons, snakes and agama lizards are among the 80 reptile species native to the country.

***Keren Kayemet* – The Jewish National Fund (JNF)** was founded
(1901) to purchase land for Jewish agricultural settlements, as well as to
carry out development, reclamation and afforestation projects in the Land
of Israel. By the time Israel became independent (1948), the JNF, with
funds collected from Jews all over the world, had bought some 240,000
acres (96,000 hectares), most of which had to be redeemed from centuries
of neglect, and had planted about 4.5 million trees on the country's rocky
hillsides. Today over 200 million trees in forests and woodlands covering
some 300,000 acres (120,000 hectares) provide Israelis with a wide range
of opportunities for outdoor recreation and appreciation of nature. While
continuing its activities of afforestation and forest maintenance, the JNF
also develops parks and recreation sites, prepares infrastructure for new
settlements, carries out various water-harvesting projects and is an active
partner in environmental conservation efforts throughout the country.

NATURE CONSERVATION

In efforts to conserve the natural environment, stringent laws for the protection of nature and wildlife have been enacted, making it illegal to pick even the most common roadside flowers. Charged with the advancement of nature preservation, the Nature Reserve Authority, together with the Society for the Protection of Nature in Israel, strives to balance the requirements of infrastructure development with protection of the landscape and natural environment. Over 150 nature reserves, established throughout the country under the Authority's supervision, encompass nearly 1,350 square miles (almost 3,500 sq. km.). About 20 have been developed for public use with visitors' centers, roads and hiking trails, attracting over two million people every year.

Hundreds of plants and animals, including the oak, palm, gazelle, ibex, leopard and vulture, are protected, and special rescue operations have been initiated to ensure the survival of a number of endangered species. Feeding stations for wolves, hyenas and foxes have been set up, as well as safe nesting sites for birds. Eggs of marine turtles are collected regularly from the Mediterranean shore and hatched in incubators; the young turtles are then returned to the sea. To prevent collisions between aircraft and the masses of birds passing over the country in spring and fall, bird migration routes are carefully monitored, and aircraft are forbidden to fly in these paths.

which once roamed the hills and deserts of the Land of Israel, into their former natural habitats. Israeli wildlife biologists search the world for these animals and, when located, have them brought to the Hai Bar reserves where they learn to cope with the environment before being set free. Animals now being raised in the country include ostriches, Persian fallow deer, oryxes, onagers and Somali wild asses.

Public awareness of nature preservation is promoted in schools and among the population at large through guided excursions, publications and information campaigns.

Inspired by a profound sense of heritage, efforts are being made to preserve and reintroduce plant and animal life which existed in biblical times and have since either disappeared from the region or are threatened with extinction. Neot Kedumim, a landscape reserve in the center of the country dedicated to collecting and conserving extant plant varieties mentioned in the Bible, has established extensive gardens with flora native to various geographical areas of the Land of Israel in ancient times. The Hai Bar wildlife projects in the Arava and on Mount Carmel were set up to reintroduce animal species,

INFRASTRUCTURE

Communications: Israel is connected to the world's major commercial, financial and academic data networks and is fully integrated into international communications systems by means of underwater cables and satellites. Telephone, telex, electronic mail and fax services are available throughout the country, providing rapid means of communication within Israel and with the rest of the world. Postal services operate throughout Israel and connect it with most countries abroad. The Philatelic Service has issued over 1,200 stamps. Many well-known Israeli artists have helped create these 'calling cards,' some of which have already attained the status of classics and are eagerly sought by collectors.

Roads: In a country of short distances like Israel, automobiles, buses and trucks are the main means of transportation. In recent years, the road network has been extensively expanded and improved to accommodate the rapid increase in the number of vehicles as well as to make even the most remote communities accessible. Currently a multilane highway, to run almost 190 miles (300 km.), is being constructed starting at Be'er Sheva in the south and branching out to Rosh Hanikra and Rosh Pina in the north. This limited-access toll road will make it possible to bypass heavily populated areas, thus easing traffic congestion and providing fast access to most areas of the country.

Railways: Israel Railways operates passenger services between Jerusalem, Tel Aviv, Haifa and Nahariya. Freight services also operate further south, serving the port of Ashdod, the cities of Ashkelon and Be'er Sheva and the mineral quarries south of Dimona. In recent years, both rail freight and passenger usage has increased. To help alleviate problems caused by increased road-traffic density, rapid rail transit services, utilizing upgraded existing tracks, are now being instituted in the Tel Aviv and Haifa areas, operated in coordination with bus feeder lines. Many outmoded coaches now in use are being replaced by modern, air-conditioned passenger cars, and up-to-date mechanical track-maintenance equipment is being put into operation.

Seaports: The ancient ports of Jaffa (Yafo), Caesarea and Acre (Akko) have been replaced by three modern deep-water harbors at Haifa, Eilat and Ashdod which serve international shipping. Haifa is today one of the largest container ports on the Mediterranean Sea as well as a busy passenger terminal. Ashdod port is used mainly for shipping goods, and the port of Eilat on the Red Sea links Israel to the southern hemisphere and the Far East. In addition, a tanker port in Ashkelon receives fuel shipments, and a direct off-loading facility for freighters supplying coal to the nearby power station operates in Hadera.

Recognizing that Israel's geographic location gives it the potential to become a transit country for passengers and goods traversing the region, the Ports and Railways Authority has designed a long-term master plan to meet future transportation needs. Among other priorities, it advocates developing a modern rail system, instititing state-of-the-art equipment in every phase of its land and sea operations and setting up a network of computer systems to control and supervise all of its services.

Airports: Ben-Gurion International Airport (a 25-minute drive from Tel Aviv, 50 minutes from Jerusalem) is Israel's main and largest air terminal. Due to rapid increases in the numbers of passenger arrivals and departures, the airport has recently been extensively enlarged. Charter flights, mainly from Europe, and domestic air travel are served by the Eilat airport in the south and small airports near Tel Aviv and Jerusalem in the center and Rosh Pina in the north.

Architecture through the Ages: The style of urban building in Israel varies greatly, from structures of past centuries, solid edifices inspired by the renowned architects of pre-World War II Europe and apartment blocks hastily constructed to house new immigrants in the early years of the state, to carefully planned residential neighborhoods, high-rise concrete and glass office buildings and luxury hotels built in the last two decades.

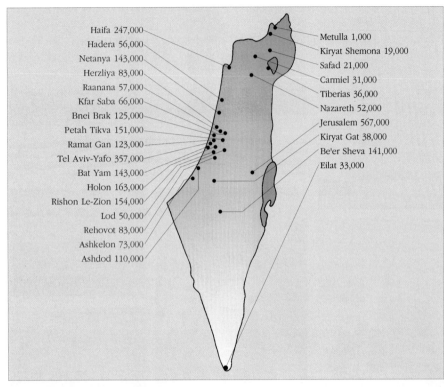

Haifa 247,000
Hadera 56,000
Netanya 143,000
Herzliya 83,000
Raanana 57,000
Kfar Saba 66,000
Bnei Brak 125,000
Petah Tikva 151,000
Ramat Gan 123,000
Tel Aviv-Yafo 357,000
Bat Yam 143,000
Holon 163,000
Rishon Le-Zion 154,000
Lod 50,000
Rehovot 83,000
Ashkelon 73,000
Ashdod 110,000

Metulla 1,000
Kiryat Shemona 19,000
Safad 21,000
Carmiel 31,000
Tiberias 36,000
Nazareth 52,000
Jerusalem 567,000
Kiryat Gat 38,000
Be'er Sheva 141,000
Eilat 33,000

Some Urban Centers: Population

URBAN LIFE

More than 90 percent of Israelis live in urban areas. Many modern towns and cities, blending the old and the new, are built on sites known since antiquity, among them Jerusalem, Safed, Be'er Sheva, Tiberias and Akko. Others such as Rehovot, Hadera, Petah Tikva and Rishon Le-Zion began as agricultural villages in the pre-state era and gradually evolved into major population centers. Development towns such as Carmiel and Kiryat Gat were built in the early years of the state to accommodate the rapid population growth generated by mass immigration, as well as to help distribute the population throughout the country and to promote a closely interlocked rural and urban economy by drawing industry and services to previously unpopulated areas.

Jerusalem, capital of Israel

Jerusalem, situated in the Judean Hills, is the capital of Israel, the seat of government and the historical, spiritual and national center of the Jewish people since King David made it the capital of his kingdom some 3,000 years ago. Sanctified by religion and tradition, by holy places and houses of worship, it is revered by Jews, Christians and Muslims the world over.

Until 1860 Jerusalem was a walled city made up of four quarters – Jewish, Muslim, Armenian and Christian. At that time, the Jews, who by then comprised the majority of its population, began to establish new neighborhoods outside the walls, forming the nucleus of modern Jerusalem. During three decades of British administration (1918–48), the city gradually changed from a neglected provincial town of the Ottoman Empire (1518–1918) into a flourishing metropolis, with many new residential neighborhoods, each reflecting the character of the particular group living there. Following the Arab onslaught against the newly established State of Israel, the city was divided (1949) under Israeli and Jordanian rule, and for the next 19 years concrete walls and barbed wire sealed off one part from the other. As a result of the assault on Jerusalem in the 1967 Six-Day War, the city was reunified.

Today Israel's largest city, Jerusalem has a population of over half a million. At once ancient and modern, it is a city of diversity, with inhabitants representing a mixture of cultures and nationalities, of religiously observant and secular lifestyles. It is a city which preserves its past and builds for the future, with carefully restored historical sites, well-landscaped green areas, modern commercial zones, industrial parks and expanding suburbs attesting to its continuity and vitality.

 Tel Aviv–Yafo, a modern city on the Mediterranean coast, is Israel's commercial and financial center as well as the focus of its cultural life. Headquartered there are most industrial and agricultural organizations, the stock exchange, major newspapers, periodicals and publishing houses. Tel Aviv, the first all-Jewish city in modern times, was founded in 1909 as a suburb of Yafo, one of the oldest urban settlements in the world. In 1934 Tel Aviv was granted municipal status, and in 1950 it was merged with Yafo, the new municipality absorbing the older town. The area around the ancient port of Yafo (Jaffa) has been developed into an artists' colony and tourist center, with galleries, restaurants and night clubs.

Haifa, on the Mediterranean Sea, rises from the coastline over the slopes of Mount Carmel. It is built on three topographical levels: the lower city, partly on land recovered from the sea, is the commercial center with harbor facilities; the middle level is an older residential area; and the top level consists of rapidly expanding modern neighborhoods with tree-lined streets, parks and pine woods, overlooking the industrial zones and sandy beaches on the shore of the wide bay below. A major deep-water port, Haifa is a focus of international trade and commerce. It also serves as the administrative center of northern Israel.

Safed, perched high in the mountains of Galilee, is a popular summer resort and tourist site, with an artists' quarter and several centuries-old synagogues. In the 16th century, Safed was the most important center of Jewish learning and creativity in the world – the gathering place of rabbis, scholars and mystics who laid down religious laws and precepts, many of which are still followed by observant Jews today.

Tiberias, on the shore of Lake Kinneret, is famous for its therapeutic hot springs. Today the town is a bustling lakeside tourist center, where archaeological remains of the past blend with modern houses and hotels. Founded in the 1st century and named for the Roman Emperor Tiberius, it became a center of Jewish scholarship and the site of a well-known rabbinical academy.

Be'er Sheva, in the northern Negev, is located at the intersection of routes leading to the Dead Sea and Eilat. It is a new city built on an ancient site, dating back to the age of the Patriarchs some 3,500 years ago. Called the 'Capital of the Negev,' Be'er Sheva is an administrative and economic center, with regional government offices and institutions of health, education and culture which serve all of southern Israel.

Eilat, the country's southernmost city, is Israel's outlet to the Red Sea and the Indian Ocean. Its modern port, believed to be located on the site of a harbor used in the time of King Solomon, handles Israel's trade with Africa and the Far East. Warm winters, spectacular underwater scenery, well-appointed beaches, water sports, luxury hotels and accessibility from Europe via direct charter flights have made Eilat a thriving, year-round tourist resort. Since the establishment of peace between Israel and Jordan (1994), joint development projects with the neighboring city of Akaba have been initiated, mainly to boost tourism in the area.

RURAL LIFE

About 9 percent of Israel's population lives in rural areas, in villages and two unique cooperative frameworks, the kibbutz and moshav, which were developed in the country in the early part of the 20th century.

Villages of various sizes are inhabited mainly by Arabs and Druze, who comprise one sixth of Israel's rural population. Land and houses are privately owned, and farmers cultivate and market their crops on an individual basis. A minority within the Arab sector, formerly nomadic Bedouin Arabs in the Negev (some 70,000 people) are currently undergoing an urbanization process, reflecting the transition from a traditional society to a settled, modern lifestyle.

The **kibbutz** is a self-contained social and economic unit in which decisions are taken by the general assembly of its members, and property and means of production are communally owned. Today 2.3 percent of the population lives in some 270 kibbutzim. Members are assigned work in different branches of the kibbutz economy; children spend most of their waking hours with their peer group in organized frameworks, from infancy through high school. Traditionally the backbone of Israel's agriculture (today producing 33 percent of the country's farm output), kibbutzim are now also engaged in industry, tourism and services.

The **moshav** is a rural settlement in which each family maintains its own farm and household. In the past cooperation extended to purchasing and marketing; today moshav farmers have chosen to be more economically independent. Some 450 moshavim, averaging about 60 families each and comprising 3.1 percent of the population, supply much of Israel's agricultural produce.

The **yishuv kehilati** is a new form of rural settlement, with each of the 50–60 existing communities containing hundreds of families. Although each family's economic life is completely independent and most members work outside the community, the level of volunteer participation of members in community life is very high. The central governing institution is the General Assembly, made up of the heads of each household, which sets and passes the community's budget at its annual meeting. Alongside management and oversight committees, a number of working groups deal with areas such as education, culture, youth, finances and the like. A paid secretariat runs the community's day-to-day affairs according to the decisions of the elected bodies. New members are accepted only with the approval of the community.

society

SOCIETY

Jewish Society

Minority Communities

Religious Freedom

...הנה מה טוב ומה נעים שבת אחים גם יחד.

(תהילים קל"ג:א')

...Behold, how good and how pleasant it is for brothers to dwell in unity.

(Psalms 133:1)

Israel is home to a widely diverse population from many ethnic, religious, cultural and social backgrounds. A new society with ancient roots, it is still coalescing and evolving today. Of its more than 5.5 million people, 81.2 percent are Jews, (over half native-born, the rest from some 70 countries around the world), 17.1 percent are Arabs (mostly Muslim) and the remaining 1.7 percent comprise Druze, Circassian and other small communities. The society is relatively young (median age 26.4 years), characterized by social and religious commitment, political ideology, economic resourcefulness and cultural creativity, all of which contribute dynamic momentum to its continuing development.

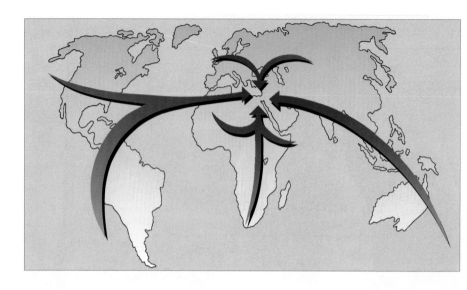

JEWISH SOCIETY
THE LONG ROAD HOME

Following their expulsion from the Land of Israel some 2,000 years ago, the Jews were dispersed to other countries, mainly in Europe, North Africa and the Middle East. Over the centuries, they established many large Jewish communities in lands near and far where they experienced long periods of growth and prosperity, but were also subjected at times to harsh discrimination, brutal pogroms and total or partial expulsions. Each wave of persecution and violence strengthened their belief in the concept of the 'ingathering of the exiles' and inspired individuals and groups to return to their ancestral homeland. The Zionist movement, founded at the end of the 19th century, transformed the concept into a way of life, and the State of Israel translated it into law, granting citizenship to every Jew wishing to settle in the country.

FORMATION OF A NEW SOCIETY

The political, economic and cultural basis of Israel's contemporary Jewish society was formed during the British Mandate period (1922–48). Ideologically motivated by Zionism, the Jewish community in the Land of Israel developed social and political institutions which exercised authority without sovereignty, with every echelon mobilized towards consolidation and growth. Volunteerism was its political spine, egalitarianism its social glue.

The attainment of political independence and the mass immigration which followed, doubling Israel's Jewish population from 650,000 to some 1.3 million in the first four years of statehood (1948–52), changed the structure and fabric of Israeli society. The resultant social grouping was composed of two main elements: a majority comprised mainly of veteran settlers and Holocaust survivors from post-war Europe; and a large minority of recent Jewish immigrants from the Islamic countries of North Africa and the Middle East. While most of the pre-state population was committed to strong ideological convictions, a pioneering spirit and a democratic way of life, many of the Jews who had lived for centuries in Arab lands adhered to a patriarchal social organization, were unfamiliar with the democratic process and the demands of a modern society, and found it difficult to integrate into Israel's rapidly developing economy.

In the late 1950s, the two groups coexisted virtually without social and cultural interaction, with the Jews of North African and Middle Eastern backgrounds expressing their frustration and alienation in anti-government protests, which, in the 1960s and 1970s, became demands for greater political participation, compensatory allocations of resources and affirmative action to help close the gap between them and mainstream Israelis. In addition to the tensions generated by the diversity of its population during these years, Israeli society was also called upon to struggle for economic independence and to defend itself against belligerent actions by Arabs across the border. Still, the common denominators of religion, historical memory and national cohesion within the Jewish society proved strong enough to meet the challenges facing it.

By the 1980s, the protest movements which had once commanded headlines became marginal, previously stigmatized groups advanced on all levels and a large percentage of all marriages were inter-ethnic. Now after a half a century of independence and with a strong economy, the society is essentially stable, attesting to a political culture based on understandings between the various social groups and committed to its essential values: a Jewish state in its ancient homeland, democratic governance, ongoing immigration and the attainment of peace with its neighbors. Nevertheless, ethnic diversity is very much a part of Israeli society, affecting all aspects of its cultural, religious and political life. The social tensions which were once thought to threaten the integrity and cohesion of the society today contribute to its pluralistic nature.

CONTINUED INGATHERING

Over the years, Israel has continued to receive new immigrants in larger and smaller numbers, coming from the free countries of the Western world as well as from areas of distress. The most recent wave of mass immigration comprises members of the large Jewish community of the former Soviet Union which struggled for years for the right to emigrate to Israel. While some 100,000 managed to come in the 1970s, since 1989 over 700,000 have settled in the country. Among the newcomers are many highly educated professionals, well-known scientists and acclaimed artists and musicians, whose expertise and talents are contributing significantly to Israel's economic, scientific, academic and cultural life.

The 1980s and 1990s witnessed the arrival of two massive airlifts of the ancient Jewish community of Ethiopia, believed to have been there since the time of King Solomon. While the transition of these 30,000 immigrants from an agrarian African environment to an industrialized Western society will take time, the eagerness of their youth to adapt will hasten the eventual absorption of this long-isolated Jewish community.

RELIGIOUS DIVERSITY

Since biblical times, the Jews have been a people with one monotheistic faith, Judaism, embodying both a religious and a national significance. By the 18th century, most of the world's Jews lived in Europe where they were confined to ghettos and had little interaction with the societies around them. Within their communities, they managed their own affairs, adhering to the body of Jewish law (*Halakhah*) which had been developed and codified by religious scholars over many centuries.

The spirit of emancipation and nationalism which swept 19th century Europe also penetrated the walls of the ghetto, generating the development of a more liberal approach to education, culture, philosophy and theology. It also gave rise to several Jewish movements, some of which developed along liberal religious lines, while others espoused national and political ideologies. As a result, many Jews, and ultimately the majority, broke from Orthodoxy and its attendant way of life, with some striving to integrate completely into the society at large.

Jewish society in Israel today is made up of observant and non-observant Jews, comprising a spectrum from the ultra-Orthodox to

those who regard themselves as secular. However, the differences between them are not clear-cut. If Orthodoxy is determined by the degree of adherence to Jewish religious laws and practices, then 20 percent of Israeli Jews fulfill all religious precepts, 60 percent follow some combination of the laws according to personal choices and ethnic traditions, and 20 percent are essentially non-observant. But as Israel was conceived as a Jewish state, the Sabbath (Saturday) and all Jewish festivals and holy days have been instituted as national holidays and are celebrated by the entire Jewish population and observed by all, to a greater or lesser extent.

Other indicators of the degree of religious adherence might be the percentage of parents choosing to give their children a religiously-oriented education or the percentage of voters casting their ballot for religious parties in national elections. The significance of such statistics, however, is uncertain, as non-observant parents may enroll their children in religious schools and many Orthodox citizens vote for non-religious political parties.

Basically, the majority may be characterized as secular Jews who manifest modern lifestyles, with varied degrees of respect for and practice of religious precepts. Within this majority are many who follow a

modified traditional way of life, with some choosing to affiliate with one of the liberal religious streams.

Within the observant minority are many who adhere to a religious way of life, regulated by Jewish religious law, while participating in the country's national life. They regard the modern Jewish state as the first step towards the coming of the Messiah and redemption of the Jewish people in the Land of Israel.

In contrast, the *Haredim* (ultra-Orthodox Jews) believe that Jewish sovereignty in the Land can be reestablished only after the coming of the Messiah. Maintaining strict adherence to Jewish religious law, they reside in separate neighborhoods, run their own schools, dress in traditional clothing, maintain distinct roles for men and women and are bound by a closely circumscribed lifestyle. Their community consists of two subgroups: a small but volatile element which does not recognize the existence of the state and isolates itself from it; and a pragmatic majority which participates in Israeli politics with the aim of strengthening the Jewish religious character of the state.

INTER-JEWISH DYNAMICS

As there is no clear separation of religion and state, a central inter-community issue has been the extent to which Israel should manifest its Jewish religious identity. While the Orthodox establishment seeks to augment religious legislation beyond the scope of personal status, over which it has exclusive jurisdiction, the non-observant sector regards this as religious coercion and an infringement on the democratic nature of the state. One of the ongoing issues focuses on the elements required to define a person as a Jew. The Orthodox sector advocates determining a Jew as one born of a Jewish mother, in strict accordance with Jewish law, while secular Jews generally support a definition based on the civil criterion of an individual's identification with Judaism. These conflicts of interest have given rise to a search for legal means to define the demarcation between religion and state. Until an overall solution is found, authority lies in an unwritten agreement, reached on the eve of Israel's independence and known as the *status quo*, which stipulates that no fundamental changes would be made in the status of religion.

KIBBUTZ SOCIETY

A unique social and economic framework based on egalitarian and communal principles, the kibbutz grew out of the country's pioneering society of the early 20th century and developed into a permanent rural way of life. Over the years, it established a prosperous economy, at first primarily agricultural, later augmented with industrial and service enterprises, and distinguished itself with its members' contributions to the establishment and building of the state.

In Israel's pre-state period and during the early years of statehood, the kibbutz assumed central functions in settlement, immigration and defense, but when these were transferred to the government, interaction between the kibbutz and Israel's mainstream decreased. Its centrality as a vanguard for social and institutional development diminished, and since the 1970s its political strength, which in the early days had resulted in overrepresentation, has declined. However, the kibbutzim's share in the national product has continued to be significantly greater than their proportion of the population.

In recent decades the kibbutz has become more introspective, emphasizing individual achievement and economic growth. In many kibbutzim, the 'do-it-ourselves' work ethic has become less rigid as the taboo on hired labor in the kibbutz has weakened, and greater numbers of non-member paid workers are being employed. At the same time, increasing numbers of kibbutz members are working outside the kibbutz, with their salary accruing to the kibbutz.

Today's kibbutz is the achievement of three generations. The founders, motivated by strong convictions and a definitive ideology, formed a society with a unique way of life. Their children, born into an existing social structure, worked hard to consolidate the economic, social and administrative basis of their community. The present generation, which grew up in a well-established society, is grappling with the challenges of contemporary life. Today, much discussion focuses on the future nature of the relationship and mutual responsibility between the individual and the kibbutz community, as well as on ramifications for the society of recent developments in technology and communications. Some fear that in adjusting to changing circumstances the kibbutz is moving dangerously far from its original principles and values; others believe that this ability to compromise and adapt is the key to its survival.

The kibbutz dining hall is more than just a place to eat: Here members enjoy festive meals on Friday evenings and holidays; here the kibbutz makes major decisions at the meetings of its General Assembly, and here hours of intense informal discussion take place during hundreds of breakfasts, lunches and suppers.

MINORITY COMMUNITIES

Over one million people, comprising 18.8 percent of Israel's population, are non-Jews. Although defined collectively as Arab citizens of Israel, they include a number of different, primarily Arabic-speaking, groups, each with distinct characteristics.

Muslim Arabs, numbering some 780,000, most of whom are Sunni, constitute 76 percent of the non-Jewish population. They reside mainly in small towns and villages, over half of them in the north of the country.

Bedouin Arabs, comprising nearly 10 percent of the Muslim population, belong to some 30 tribes, most of them scattered over a wide area in the south. Formerly nomadic shepherds, the Bedouin are currently in transition from a tribal social framework to a permanently settled society and are gradually entering Israel's labor force.

Christian Arabs, who constitute Israel's second largest minority group of some 150,000, live mainly in urban areas, including Nazareth, Shfar'am and Haifa. Although many denominations are nominally represented, the majority are affiliated with the Greek Catholic (42 percent), Greek Orthodox (32 percent) and Roman Catholic (16 percent) churches.

The Druze, some 80,000 Arabic-speakers living in 22 villages in northern Israel, constitute a separate cultural, social and religious community. While the Druze religion is not accessible to outsiders, one known aspect of its philosophy is the concept of *taqiyya*, which calls for complete loyalty by its adherents to the government of the country in which they reside.

The Circassians, comprising some 3,000 people concentrated in two northern villages, are Sunni Muslims, although they share neither the Arab origin nor the cultural background of the larger Islamic community. While maintaining a distinct ethnic identity, they participate in Israel's economic and national affairs without assimilating either into Jewish society or into the general Muslim community.

ARAB COMMUNITY LIFE

Arab migrations in and out of the country fluctuated in response to prevailing economic conditions. Late in the 19th century when Jewish immigration stimulated economic growth, many Arabs were attracted to the area by its employment opportunities, higher wages and better living conditions.

The majority of Israel's Arab population live in self-contained towns and villages in four main areas: Galilee, including the city of Nazareth, the central area between Hadera and Petah Tikva, and the Negev; others reside in mixed urban centers such as Jerusalem, Akko, Haifa, Lod, Ramle and Yafo.

Israel's Arab community constitutes mainly a working-class sector in a predominantly middle-class society, a politically peripheral group in a highly centralized state and an Arabic-speaking minority in a Hebrew-speaking majority. Essentially non-

assimilating, the community's separate existence is facilitated through the use of Arabic, Israel's second official language; a separate Arab/Druze school system; Arabic mass media, literature and theater; and maintenance of independent Muslim, Druze and Christian denominational courts which adjudicate matters of personal status. While customs of the past are still part of daily life, a gradual weakening of tribal and patriarchal authority, the effects of compulsory education and participation in Israel's democratic process are rapidly affecting traditional outlooks and lifestyles. Concurrently the status of Israeli Arab women has been significantly liberalized by legislation stipulating equal rights for women and prohibition of polygamy and child marriage.

Accounting for over 10 percent of eligible voters, the political involvement of the Arab sector is manifested in national and municipal elections. Arab citizens run the political and administrative affairs of their own municipalities and represent Arab interests through their elected representatives in the Knesset (Israel's parliament), who operate in the political arena to promote the status of minority groups and their share of national benefits.

Since Israel's establishment (1948), Arab citizens have been exempted from compulsory service in the Israel Defense Forces (IDF) out of consideration for their family, religious and cultural affiliations with the Arab world (with which Israel had a long dispute), as well as concern over possible dual loyalties. At the same time, volunteer military service is encouraged, with some choosing this option every year. Since 1957, at the request of their community leaders, IDF service has been mandatory for Druze and Circassian men, while the number of Bedouin joining the career army increases steadily.

ARAB-JEWISH DYNAMICS

Israel's Arab citizens, who constitute one-seventh of Israel's population and one-seventh of the Palestinian people, exist on the margins of the conflicting worlds of Jews and Palestinians. However, while remaining a segment of the Palestinian people in culture and identity and disputing Israel's identification as a Jewish state, they see their future tied to Israel. In the process, they have adopted Hebrew as a second language and Israeli culture as an extra layer in their lives. At the same time, they strive to attain a higher degree of participation in national life, greater integration into the economy and more benefits for their own towns and villages.

Development of intergroup relations between Israel's Arabs and Jews has been hindered by deeply-rooted differences in religion, values and political beliefs. However, though coexisting as two self-segregated communities, over the years they have come to accept each other, acknowledging the uniqueness and aspirations of each community and participating in a growing number of joint endeavors.

PLURALISM AND SEGREGATION

As a multi-ethnic, multi-cultural, multi-religious and multi-lingual society, Israel has a high level of informal segregation patterns. While groups are not separated by official policy, a number of different sectors within the society are somewhat segregated and maintain their strong cultural, religious, ideological and/or ethnic identity.

However, despite a fairly high degree of social cleavage some economic disparities and an often overheated political life, the society is relatively balanced and stable. The moderate level of social conflict between the different groups, notwithstanding an inherent potential for social unrest, can be attributed to the country's judicial and political systems, which represent strict legal and civic equality.

Thus, Israel is not a melting pot society, but rather more of a mosaic made up of different population groups coexisting in the framework of a democratic state.

RELIGIOUS FREEDOM

The Declaration of the Establishment of the State of Israel (1948) guarantees freedom of religion for all. Each religious community is free, by law and in practice, to exercise its faith, to observe its holidays and weekly day of rest and to administer its internal affairs. Each has its own religious council and courts, recognized by law and with jurisdiction over all religious affairs and matters of personal status such as marriage and divorce. Each has its own unique places of worship, with traditional rituals and special architectural features developed over the centuries.

Synagogue: Traditional Jewish Orthodox worship requires a minyan (quorum of ten adult males). Prayers take place three times daily. Men and women are seated separately, and heads are covered. Services may be led by a rabbi, cantor or congregant. The rabbi is not a priest or an intermediary with God, but a teacher. The focal point in the synagogue is the Holy Ark, which faces the Temple Mount in Jerusalem and contains the Torah scrolls. A prescribed weekly portion is read cyclically throughout the year. Services are particularly festive on the Sabbath (Saturday, the Jewish day of rest) and holidays.

Mosque: Muslim prayers take place five times daily. Men and women pray separately. Shoes are removed and a ritual ablution may be performed. Muslims pray facing Mecca in Saudi Arabia, the direction of which is indicated by a *mihrab* (niche) in the mosque wall. Services are performed by an *imam*, a Muslim prayer leader. On Friday, the traditional Muslim day of rest, a public sermon is usually preached.

Church: The form and frequency of Christian services vary according to denomination, but all observe Sunday, the day of rest, with special rituals. Services are conducted by a priest or minister. Men and women pray together. Men usually bare their heads, women may cover them. Services are often accompanied by music and choral singing. Traditionally, churches are cruciform in shape.

Holy Places:

Each site and shrine is administered by its own religious authority, and freedom of access and worship is ensured by law.

Jewish: The Kotel, the Western ('Wailing') Wall, last remnant of the retaining wall of the Second Temple, and the Temple Mount, in Jerusalem; Rachel's Tomb, Tomb of the Patriarchs in the Cave of Machpela, in Hebron; tombs of Maimonides (Rambam) in Tiberias, Rabbi Shimon Bar Yohai in Meron and many others.

Islamic: *Haram ash-Sharif* building complex on the Temple Mount, including the Dome of the Rock and *Al-Aksa* mosque, in Jerusalem; Tomb of the Patriarchs, in Hebron; *El-Jazzar* mosque, in Akko.

Christian: Via Dolorosa, Room of the Last Supper, Church of the Holy Sepulchre and other sites of Jesus' passion and crucifixion, in Jerusalem; Church of the Nativity, in Bethlehem; Church of the Annunciation, in Nazareth; Mount of Beatitudes, Tabgha and Capernaum, near Sea of Galilee (Lake Kinneret).

Druze: *Nebi Shuieb* (tomb of Jethro, father-in-law of Moses), near Horns of Hittin in Galilee.

Baha'i (independent world religion founded in Persia, mid-19th century): Baha'i world center, Shrine of the Bab, in Haifa; Shrine of Baha'u'llah, prophet-founder of the Baha'i faith, near Akko.

The **Karaites**, a Jewish sect dating back to the 8th century, profess strict adherence to the Torah (Five Books of Moses) as the sole source of religious law. Although considered a faction in Judaism and not a separate community, the Karaites maintain their own religious courts and tend to marry among themselves. Some 15,000 live in Israel today, mainly in Ramle, Ashdod and Be'er Sheva.

The **Samaritans** regard themselves as true Jews, faithful only to the Torah and its immediate sequel, the Book of Joshua. Mount Gerizim in Samaria is their holy site, where they believe Abraham tried to sacrifice Isaac and Solomon built the First Temple. Claiming descent from the 10 lost Israelite tribes, the nearly 600 remaining members of the ancient Samaritan people live today in two localities; about half in the village of Kiryat Luza near the peak of 'the mountain,' and the other half, who are Israeli citizens, live in their own mini-neighborhood in Holon near Tel Aviv. They speak Arabic in daily life and use an archaic form of Hebrew in their liturgy. So far as is known, there are no Samaritans anywhere else in the world.

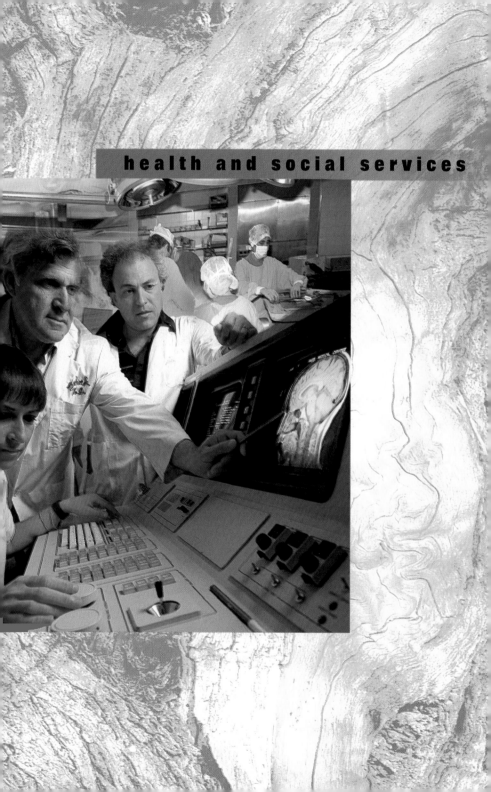

HEALTH AND SOCIAL SERVICES

HEALTH SERVICES

MEDICAL RESEARCH

ENVIRONMENTAL HAZARDS

SHARING BEYOND BORDERS

SOCIAL SERVICES

SOCIAL INSURANCE

VOLUNTARY SERVICES

כל ישראל ערבין זה בזה.
(שבועות ל"ט א')

■

All Israel is responsible
for one another.
(Babylonian Talmud, Shavuot 39a)

Israel's high standards of health services, top-quality medical resources and research, modern hospital facilities and an impressive ratio of physicians and specialists to population are reflected in the country's low infant mortality rate (7.5 per 1,000 live births) and long life expectancy (79.1 years for women, 75.3 for men). Health care for all, from infancy to old age, is ensured by law and the national expenditure on health (8.2 percent of the GNP) compares favorably with that of other developed countries.

HEALTH SERVICES

The foundation of the health system, including a network of medical services for prevention, diagnosis and treatment, was laid during the pre-state period by the Jewish community and the British Mandate authorities, which administered the country during that time (1918-48). Thus when the State of Israel was established, a well-developed medical infrastructure was already functioning, immunization was standard procedure and frameworks for improving environmental conditions were operative.

However, in the early years of statehood, the health services had to readdress some of the problems previously overcome in order to cope with the health needs of hundreds of thousands of refugees from postwar Europe and various Arab countries. This challenge was met through an intense national effort involving provision of special services as well as a far-reaching plan of health education and preventive medicine.

The country's population is served by an extensive medical network

A Long-Standing Tradition: In the 19th century, diseases such as dysentery, malaria, typhus and trachoma were rampant in the Land of Israel, then a backward and neglected part of the Ottoman Empire. To provide health services for the Jewish population of the Old City of Jerusalem, a number of clinics, set up by European Jewish communities, extended free medical services for those unable to pay and were famous for their dedicated care under difficult circumstances. These clinics expanded to become hospitals: Bikur Holim (est. 1843), Misgav Ladach (est. 1888) and Shaare Zedek (est. 1902), which still function today, offering up-to-date services with modern medical technology. The Hadassah Medical Center in Jerusalem, with schools of medicine, nursing and pharmacology and two modern hospitals, traces its beginning to two nurses who were sent to Jerusalem in 1913 by the Hadassah Women's Zionist Organization of America.

comprising hospitals, outpatient clinics and centers for preventive medicine and rehabilitation. Hospital care includes highly advanced procedures and techniques, from in vitro fertilization, CAT scans and complicated brain surgery to bone marrow and organ transplants.

Mother-and-child care centers, for women during pregnancy and children from birth to early childhood, offer prenatal examinations, early detection of mental and physical handicaps, immunizations, regular pediatric check-ups and health education.

HOSPITAL BEDS PER 1,000 PERSONS

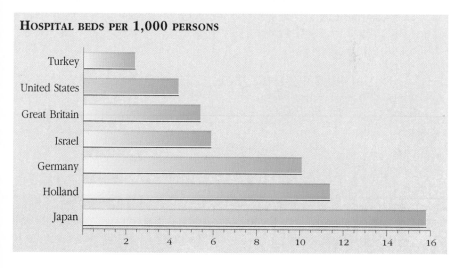

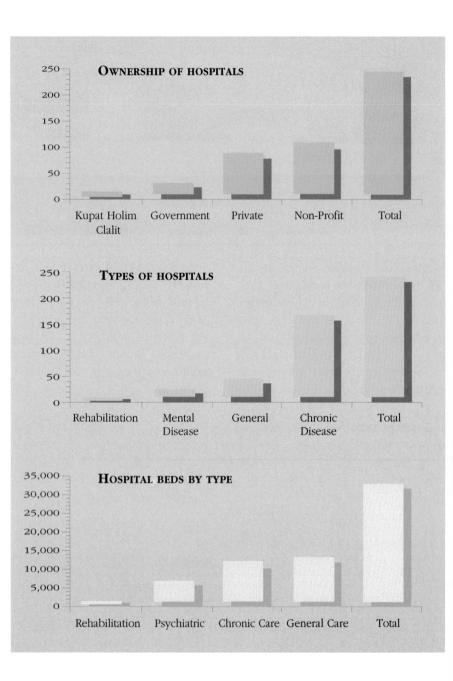

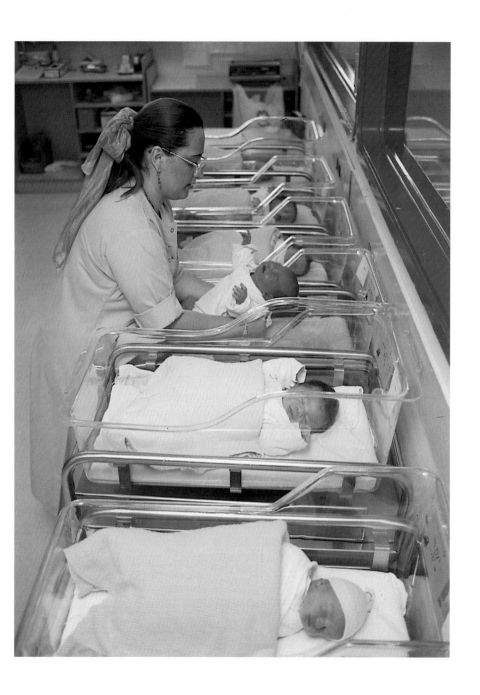

ADMINISTRATION AND STRUCTURE

Responsibility for all health services lies with the Ministry of Health, which prepares legislation and oversees its implementation; controls medical standards nationwide; maintains food and drug quality standards; licenses medical personnel; promotes medical research; evaluates health services; and supervises the planning and construction of hospitals. The Ministry also acts as a public health agency for environmental and preventive medicine.

HEALTH PERSONNEL

Israel's approximately 27,000 physicians pursue their profession as members of hospital staffs and neighborhood clinics as well as in private practice. About half of the country's 47,000 nurses are registered (of whom 6 percent also have a university degree), while the rest are practical nurses.

Training for medical professions is offered at four medical schools, two schools of dentistry, one of pharmacology and some 20 nursing schools, four of which grant academic degrees. Courses for physiotherapists, occupational therapists and nutritionists, as well as for x-ray and laboratory technicians, are available at a number of institutions.

HEALTH INSURANCE

The National Insurance Law provides for a standardized basket of medical services, including hospitalization, for all residents of Israel. Medical services are supplied by the country's four comprehensive health insurance schemes, which must accept all applicants regardless of age or state of health.

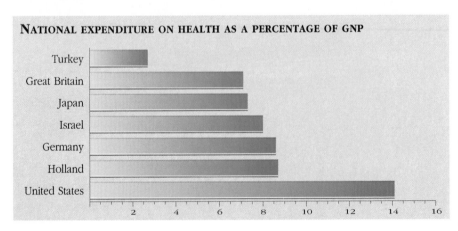

NATIONAL EXPENDITURE ON HEALTH AS A PERCENTAGE OF GNP

Magen David Adom, Israel's emergency medical service, provides a network of first aid stations, a nationwide blood donor program, blood banks and first aid courses, a public ambulance

service, which includes intensive care units. The organization functions with the help of 4,500 volunteers, many of them high school students, who serve at some 40 branches throughout the country.

The main sources of funding are a monthly health insurance tax of up to 4.8 percent of income, collected by the National Insurance Institute, and employer participation in the cost of insurance for their employees. The insurance schemes are reimbursed according to a weighted average number of insured persons, calculated by age, distance of home from a health facility and other criteria determined by the Ministry of Health.

HEALTH PROBLEMS

Israel's health problems are similar to those prevailing in the Western world. Since cancer and heart diseases account for two thirds of deaths, the study of these illnesses has become a national priority Also of great concern are medical care for the aging, problems arising from environmental changes and conditions emanating from current lifestyles, as well as traffic and occupational accidents. Health education programs are being widely utilized to inform the public of the need to stop habits such as smoking and overeating, as well as lack of physical exercise, which have proved detrimental to health. Campaigns are also run frequently to increase workers' and drivers' awareness of potential dangers.

MEDICAL RESEARCH

Israel's well-developed infrastructure of medical and paramedical research and bio-engineering capabilities facilitates a wide range of scientific inquiry.

Research is carried out by the medical schools and various government institutes and laboratories, as well as by R&D departments of companies in the pharmaceutical, bio-engineering, food processing and medical equipment industries. The country's high-level facilities are recognized throughout the world, with regular contacts maintained on a reciprocal basis with major medical and scientific research centers abroad. Israel is frequently the host venue for international conferences on a wide variety of medical topics.

MEDICAL TECHNOLOGY

Sophisticated technology has become an integral part of modern diagnostic and treatment procedures in Israel. Close cooperation between medical research institutions and industry has led to significant progress in the development of special medical equipment. Among others, Israel's CAT labs and advanced microcomputer-supported devices, essential for accurate diagnosis and effective treatment in critical situations, are exported worldwide. Israel has pioneered the development and use of laser surgical instruments, as well as a variety of electronic medical equipment, including computerized monitoring systems and other life-saving and pain-relieving devices.

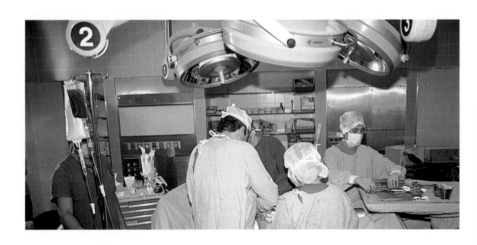

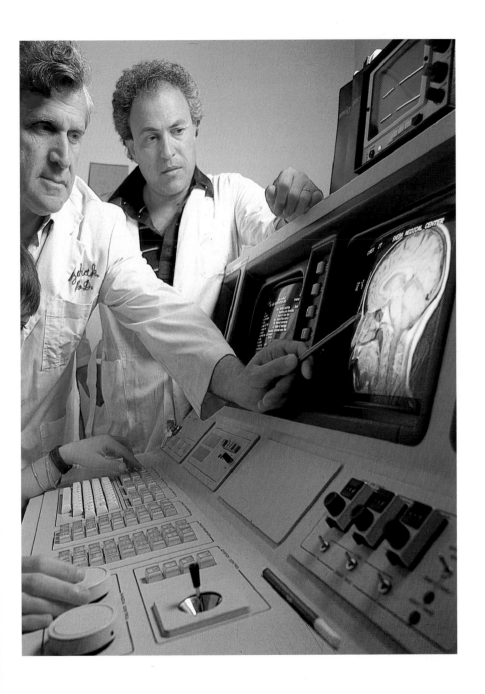

ENVIRONMENTAL HAZARDS

Environmental and health hazards have been generated by rapid population growth and steady expansion of agricultural and industrial activities. More than 70 percent of Israel's industry is concentrated along the narrow coastal zone where meteorological conditions are unfavorable for the dispersal of pollutants. To combat pollution of the Mediterranean and Red Sea coastlines, Israel has adopted a multifaceted program of legislation, enforcement, beach and shore clean-up and international activities, primarily within the framework of the Mediterranean Action Plan.

Under conditions of water scarcity and intensive development, the degradation of water quality constitutes a critical problem. The main causes of groundwater pollution are chemical fertilizers, pesticides, seawater intrusion and domestic and industrial wastewater. High priority has been given to wastewater treatment to safeguard environmental and public health and to develop an additional water source for agricultural irrigation. A rehabilitation program for polluted streams has been initiated with the aim of transforming them into vital freshwater resources with ecological and recreational value. Water quality in streams is routinely monitored, while the potability of drinking water is strictly supervised.

Factors affecting air quality include energy production, transportation and industry. In response to alarming levels of pollution in highly industrialized urban areas, primarily along the coastal plain, a comprehensive new program for the management of air resources has been launched, which includes instituting emission standards and expanding the national air monitoring system. The use of low-sulfur coal and oil for energy production has helped reduce concentrations of sulfur oxides considerably, but pollutant emissions linked to increased vehicular traffic have risen significantly. New measures, including lead-free gasoline and catalytic converters, should help combat pollution from this source.

Israel faces an increasing solid waste problem resulting from rapid growth in population, industry and consumption. Hundreds of poorly-operated dumps generate health and environmental hazards. To overcome this problem, Israel is implementing a plan to shut down illegal dumps and replace them with a few environmentally-safe landfills, as well as facilitating a shift to low- and non-waste technology, as stipulated in its recently-enacted recycling law.

Safe management of hazardous substances is spelled out in legislation enacted to provide "cradle to grave" administration, including licensing, regulation and supervision over various aspects of their production, use and handling. Enforcement of the legislation and implementation of Israel's new national contingency plan for dealing with hazardous substances accidents should minimize potential dangers to health and the environment.

In addition to regulatory measures and education as essential components of its environmental policy, Israel now also offers financial grants to companies which invest in monitoring and pollution treatment facilities and in environment-friendly technologies and materials.

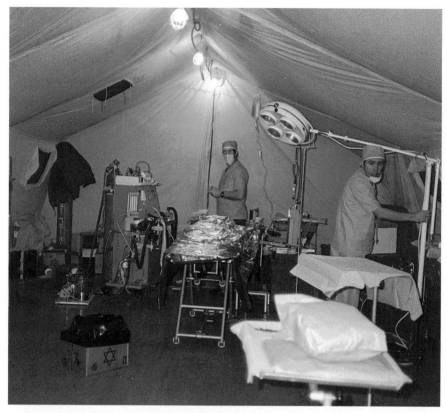

An Israeli field hospital in earthquake-devastated Armenia

SHARING BEYOND BORDERS

In accordance with the belief that proper medical care is a universal right transcending barriers of ideology and political borders, Israel's hospitals are open to all seeking their expertise. Over the years, patients have come for specialized treatment from all over the world, including countries with which Israel has no diplomatic relations.   In many parts of Asia and Africa, Israeli doctors and nurses are providing assistance in treating diseases which have been virtually eradicated in developed countries, and share their skills with local medical personnel on exchange programs, some held under the auspices of the World Health Organization.   Israeli medical teams also participate in relief efforts in disaster areas.

Health Tourism: Israel has become a popular destination for patients around the world suffering from chronic conditions such as rheumatism, psoriasis and asthma. Many benefit from special treatments in the hot springs at Tiberias, the mineral-rich waters of the Dead Sea or the dry climate of Arad, a modern city in the Negev desert.

SOCIAL SERVICES

Israel's comprehensive welfare system is based on legislation which provides for a broad range of national and community services. Care of the elderly; support programs for single parents, children and youth; prevention and treatment of alcoholism and drug abuse; and assistance for new immigrants comprise a large part of available social services. Correctional services encompass probation frameworks, remedial programs for school dropouts, and residential and observational services for youth in distress. Sheltered workshops and employment counseling are among the rehabilitation services provided for the blind and physically disabled. The mentally retarded are cared for through various residential and community-based programs.

ADMINISTRATION

Under the Social Welfare Law (1958), municipalities and local authorities are required to maintain a department responsible for the delivery of social services, 75 percent of whose budget comes from the Ministry of Labor and Social Affairs. Nationwide services such as adoption, probation frameworks and residential institutions for the mentally retarded are funded and run by the Ministry. The Ministry determines policy, initiates legislation, enacts regulations for the operation of social services and supervises those offered by public and private organizations.

SOCIAL SERVICE PERSONNEL

Schools of social work available in most universities offer graduate and postgraduate training, combining theoretical study with field work. Government-operated programs provide training at centers throughout the country for child care staff and social work aides, as well as in-service training for social work professionals. Community and case workers are employed in various contexts, including social service bureaus, community centers, immigrant absorption facilities, mother-and-child-care centers, schools, factories and hospitals.

SERVICES SUPPLIED BY THE MINISTRY OF LABOR AND SOCIAL AFFAIRS

Personal & Social Services

Rehabilitation Services for the Disabled

Services for the Mentally Handicapped

Special Services

Youth Development and Correction

SENIOR CITIZENS

Care and services for the elderly have become a major component of Israel's health and social service capabilities. While the total population has increased six-fold since the country's establishment, the number of senior citizens (age 65+) has increased 17-fold, now representing nearly 10 percent of Israel's 5.6 million inhabitants. Much of this growth has been due to mass immigration, which peaked during the 1950s and again in the 1990s, when nearly 700,000 (mainly from the countries of the former Soviet Union) arrived, more than 12 percent of them aged 65 and over. Since only about 5 percent of Israel's aged were born in the country, many had neither the time nor the opportunity to learn Hebrew, be absorbed in the work force or establish a secure economic foundation for their old age. Thus many of Israel's elderly, some 13 percent of whom are disabled, is dependant upon family and community resources.

With planning and supervision under the aegis of the Ministry of Labor and Social Affairs, delivery of services is channeled through the social service departments of the local authorities. Community-based services for senior citizens, which aim to preserve their independence at home, include assessment of needs by a social worker, assisting families caring for an aged person, senior citizens' clubs, meals-on-wheels, sheltered housing, day-care, medical equipment and transportation. Emphasis is placed on services for high-risk groups, such as people without family or adequate incomes.

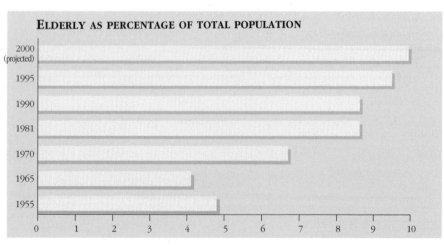

ELDERLY AS PERCENTAGE OF TOTAL POPULATION

About 6,000 homebound elderly receive 90,000 prepared meals at home each month, through The Lifeline for the Old *in Jerusalem.*

Disabled elderly are entitled to 10 to 16 weekly hours of individual home nursing care.

Handmade articles for sale are produced at this sheltered workshop for the elderly and disabled run by The Lifeline for the Old *in Jerusalem.*

Some 70,000 golden agers enjoy social activities at 700 senior citizens' clubs run by community centers and voluntary associations throughtout the country.

SOCIAL INSURANCE

The National Insurance Law (1954) grants the population a wide range of benefits which are provided by the National Insurance Institute (NII), an autonomous body operating under the aegis of the Ministry of Labor and Social Affairs. Its activities are financed by obligatory payments from employers, employees and self-employed persons, in addition to government budget allocations. The government's income maintenance policy is carried out by the NII with supplementary assistance to families and individuals whose income is below the determined minimum. Universal child allowances boost family incomes, especially for families with four or more children. An amendment to the National Insurance Law provides long-term care for elderly persons dependent on daily help, either at home or in residential facilities. The NII also administers Israel's national health insurance program.

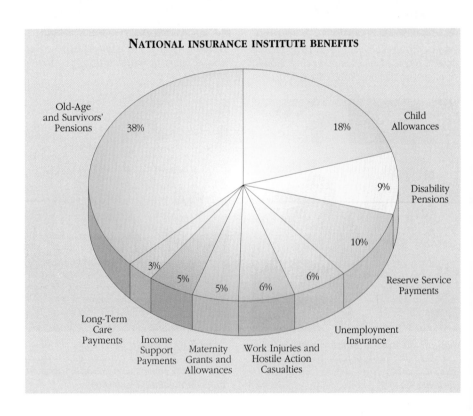

NATIONAL INSURANCE INSTITUTE BENEFITS

Old-Age and Survivors' Pensions — 38%
Child Allowances — 18%
Disability Pensions — 9%
Reserve Service Payments — 10%
Unemployment Insurance — 6%
Work Injuries and Hostile Action Casualties — 6%
Maternity Grants and Allowances — 5%
Income Support Payments — 5%
Long-Term Care Payments — 3%

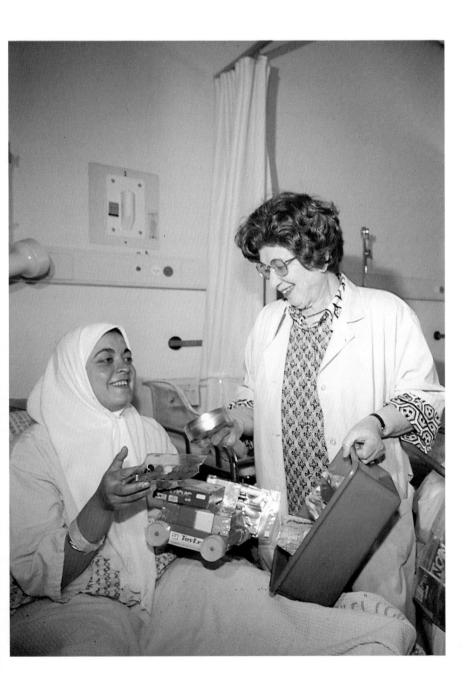

VOLUNTARY SERVICES

Several hundred public voluntary bodies complement national and local health and social services with a wide variety of organizations, ranging from hospital auxiliaries and rehabilitation agencies to immigrant associations geared to helping newcomers adjust to life in Israel. Additional groups address prevailing problems such as alcoholism, rape and battered women as well as drug and child abuse; still others deal with social issues like the status of women, environmental conservation and consumer rights, or with interests specific to a given group or locality. Campaigns by voluntary groups, including occasional national telethons, to collect funds for causes ranging from facilities for the physically and mentally handicapped to cancer research and soldiers' welfare are a regular feature of Israeli life. The well-being of people in many sectors of the population has been significantly improved due to the activities of thousands of volunteers, comprising Israelis from all walks of life, men and women, young and old.

education

EDUCATION

CHALLENGES

PRESCHOOL EDUCATION

SCHOOL SYSTEM

SECONDARY EDUCATION

HIGHER EDUCATION

ADULT EDUCATION

SPORTS

אין העולם מתקיים אלא בשל הבל
פיהן של תינוקות של בית רבן.
(שבת, קי"ט ב')

The very world rests on the
breath of a child in the
schoolhouse.
(Babylonian Talmud: Shabbat, 119b)

Education in Israel is a precious legacy. Following the tradition of past generations, education continues to be a fundamental value in Israel's society and is recognized as the key to its future. The educational system aims to prepare children to become responsible members of a democratic, pluralistic society in which people from different ethnic, religious, cultural and political backgrounds coexist. It is based on Jewish values, love of the land and the principles of liberty and tolerance. It seeks to impart a high level of knowledge, with an emphasis on scientific and technological skills essential for the country's continued development.

CHALLENGES

When the State of Israel was founded (1948), a fully functioning education system already existed, developed and maintained by the pre-state Jewish community, with Hebrew, which had been revived for daily speech at the end of the 19th century, the main language of instruction.

However, since shortly after the establishment of the state, the education system has faced the enormous challenge of integrating large numbers of immigrant children from over 70 countries – some coming with their parents, others alone – thereby fulfilling Israel's *raison d'être* as the historic homeland of the Jewish people. The mass immigration of the 1950s, mainly from postwar Europe and Arab countries, was succeeded in the 1960s by a large influx of Jews from North Africa. In the 1970s, the first sizable immigration of Soviet Jews arrived, followed intermittently by smaller groups. Since the dissolution of the Soviet Union in 1989, well over half a million Russian Jews have made their home in Israel, with tens of thousands more still arriving each year. In two mass movements, in 1984 and 1991, almost the entire Jewish community of Ethiopia was brought to the country. Over the years, many Jews from the Americas and other parts of the free world have also settled in Israel.

In addition to meeting urgent demands for more classrooms and teachers, special tools and methods have had to be developed to help absorb youngsters from many cultural backgrounds into the school population. Programs designed specifically to meet the needs of the newcomers include preparation of appropriate curricular aids and short-term classes to introduce immigrant pupils to subjects not learned in their countries of origin such as the Hebrew language and Jewish history. Special courses were initiated to train teachers to deal with immigrant youngsters, and retraining courses for immigrant teachers have facilitated their employment in the education system.

At the same time, the Ministry of Education, Culture and Sport, in cooperation with schools of education at the country's universities, is involved in an ongoing process of bringing educational standards in line with modern pedagogic practices such as mandating gender equality, upgrading teacher status, broadening humanistic curricula and promoting scientific and technological studies. A key aspect of its policy is to provide equal opportunities in education for all children and to increase the number of pupils passing matriculation examinations.

PERCENTAGE OF 12TH GRADE STUDENTS IN 17-18 YEAR-OLD POPULATION

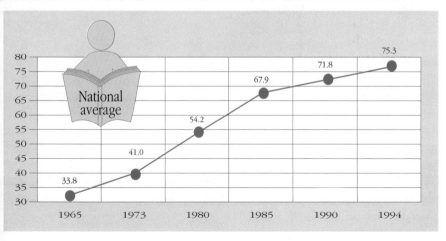

PRESCHOOL EDUCATION

Education in Israel begins at a very young age in order to provide children with an augmented 'head start,' particularly in terms of socialization and language development.

Many two-year-olds and almost all three- and four-year-olds attend some kind of preschool framework. Most programs are sponsored by local authorities, some within day-care centers operated by women's organizations; others are privately owned. The Ministry of Education allocates special resources for preschool education in disadvantaged areas.

Kindergarten for five-year-olds is free and compulsory. The curriculum aims to teach fundamental skills, including language and numerical concepts, to foster cognitive and creative capacities and to promote social abilities. The curricula of all preschools are guided and supervised by the Ministry of Education to ensure a solid and well-rounded foundation for future learning.

NATIONAL EXPENDITURE ON EDUCATION IN ISRAEL
per pupil in Israeli Shekels

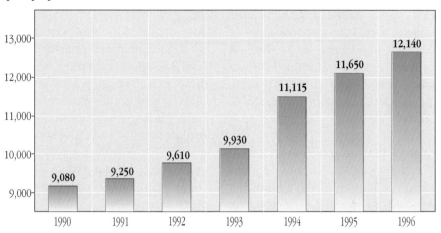

SCHOOL SYSTEM

School attendance is mandatory from age 6 to 16 and free to age 18. Formal education starts in primary school (grades 1-6) and continues with intermediate school (grades 7-9) and secondary school (grades 10-12). About nine percent of the school population aged 13-18 attends boarding schools.

The multi-cultural nature of Israel's society is accommodated within the framework of the education system. Accordingly, schools are divided into four groups: **state schools**, attended by the majority of pupils; **state religious schools**, which emphasize Jewish studies, tradition and observance; **Arab and Druze schools**, with instruction in Arabic and special focus on Arab and Druze history, religion and culture; and **private schools**, which operate under various religious and international auspices.

In recent years, with the growing concern of parents over the orientation of their children's education, some new schools have been founded, which reflect the philosophies and beliefs of specific groups of parents and educators.

CURRICULUM

Most hours of the school day are devoted to compulsory academic studies. While the subject matter to be covered is uniform throughout the system, each school may choose from a wide range of study units and teaching materials, provided by the Ministry of Education, which best suit the needs of its faculty and pupil population. With the aim of enhancing pupils' understanding of their society, each year a special topic of national importance is studied in depth. Themes have included democratic values, the Hebrew language, immigration, Jerusalem, peace and industry.

ADMINISTRATION AND STRUCTURE

The Ministry of Education is responsible for school curricula, educational standards, supervision of teaching personnel and construction of school buildings. Local authorities are charged with school maintenance as well as with acquisition of equipment and supplies. Teaching personnel at the kindergarten and primary school level are Ministry employees, while those in the upper grades are employed by local authorities, which receive funding from the Ministry according to the size of the school population. The government finances 72 percent of education, while the rest comes from local authorities and other sources.

NUMBER OF PUPILS PER COMPUTER TERMINAL

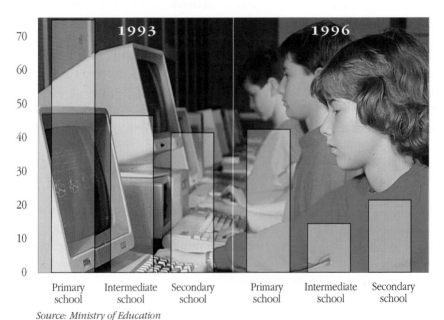

Source: *Ministry of Education*

AVERAGE NUMBER OF WEEKLY CLASSROOM HOURS
(including administrative hours)

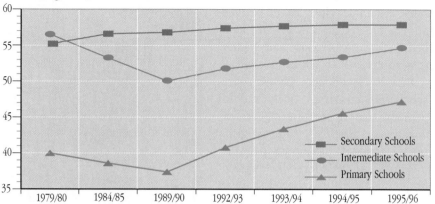

EDUCATION FOR EXCEPTIONAL CHILDREN
Gifted children, who rank in the top three percent of their class and have passed qualifying tests, participate in enrichment programs, ranging from full-time special schools to extracurricular courses. A classroom for the gifted is characterized by the level of its students and its studies, with emphasis not only on imparting knowledge and understanding, but also on applying the concepts mastered to other disciplines. Children in these programs learn to research and handle new material independently.

Children with physical, mental and learning disabilties are placed in appropriate frameworks according to the nature of their handicap, to help them eventually achieve maximum integration into the social and vocational life of their community. Thus some are taken care of in special settings, while others attend regular schools where they may be assigned to self-contained groups or to mainstream classes with supplementary tutoring. Responsibility for their well-being is shared by health care personnel, psychologists, social workers and special education professionals, as well as by the family and various community support groups. A committee constituted by law and appointed by the Minister of Education determines the eligibility of handicapped children for special education programs and facilities, which are free from age 3 to 21.

SECONDARY EDUCATION

The majority of secondary schools offer academic curricula in science and in the humanities leading to a matriculation certificate and higher education.

Certain secondary schools offer specialized curricula which lead to a matriculation certificate and/or vocational diploma. Technological schools train technicians and practical engineers on three levels, with some preparing for higher education, some studying towards a vocational diploma and others acquiring practical skills. Agricultural schools, usually in a residential setting, supplement basic studies with subjects relating to agronomy. Military preparatory schools, in two different settings, train future career personnel and technicians in specific fields required by the Israel Defense Forces; both programs are residential, one open to boys only, the other is coeducational. Yeshiva high schools, mainly boarding schools, with separate frameworks for boys and girls, complement their secular curricula with intensive religious studies and promote observance of tradition as well as a Jewish way of life. Comprehensive schools offer studies in a variety of vocations, ranging from bookkeeping to mechanics, electronics, hotel trades, graphic design and more.

Youth not attending one of the above schools are subject to the Apprenticeship Law, requiring them to study for a trade at an approved

vocational school. Apprenticeship programs are provided by the Ministry of Labor in schools affiliated with vocational networks. Lasting three to four years, these programs consist of two years of classroom study followed by one/two years during which students study three days a week and work at their chosen trade on the other days. Trades range from hairstyling and cooking to mechanics and word processing.

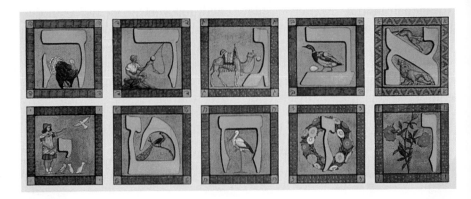

HIGHER EDUCATION

Higher education plays a pivotal role in the economic and social development of the country. Almost a quarter of a century before the state came into being, the Technion – Israel Institute of Technology in Haifa was opened (1924) to train engineers and architects needed for the rebuilding of the country, and the Hebrew University of Jerusalem was founded (1925) as a center of higher learning for youth in the Land of Israel and to attract Jewish students and scholars from abroad. When Israel attained independence in (1948), enrollment at the two universities totaled about 1,600. Today about 149,000 students attend the country's institutions of higher learning. Of these 97,000 attend universities and 28,000 are enrolled in colleges, while some 24,000 participate in courses through the Open University.

Accorded full academic and administrative freedom, Israel's institutions of higher education are open to all those who meet their academic standards. New immigrants and students lacking the necessary qualifications may attend a special preparatory program, which upon successful completion enables them to apply for admission.

COUNCIL FOR HIGHER EDUCATION

Institutions of higher education operate under the authority of the Council for Higher Education, which is headed by the Minister of Education, Culture and Sport and includes academics, community representatives and a student representative. It grants accreditation, authorizes the awarding of academic degrees and advises the government on the development and financing of higher education and scientific research.

The Planning and Grants Committee, composed of four senior academics from different fields and two public figures from the business or industrial sectors, is the intermediary body between the government and the institutions of higher education regarding financial matters, submitting budget proposals to both bodies and allocating the approved budget. Public funds provide 70 percent of the budget for higher education, 20 percent derives from tuition and the rest from various private sources. The Committee also promotes cooperation among the various institutions.

STUDENTS

Most Israeli students are over age 21 when they begin their studies, due to three years compulsory military service for men and almost two years for women. Until the early 1960s, students pursued higher education mainly to acquire knowledge, while in recent years they have been more career-oriented, with larger numbers enrolled in the wide range of professional studies now offered. At present, well over half of Israelis in the 20-24 age group are enrolled in one of the country's institutions of post-secondary or higher education.

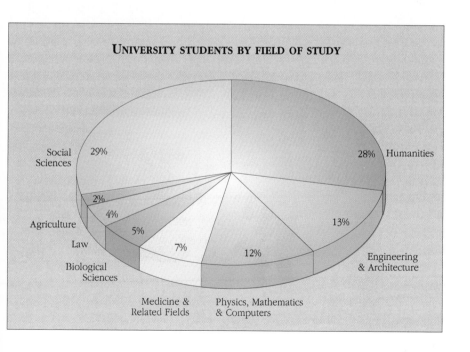

UNIVERSITY STUDENTS BY FIELD OF STUDY

Social Sciences 29% — Humanities 28% — 2% — 4% — Agriculture — 5% — Law — Biological Sciences — 7% — Medicine & Related Fields — 12% — Physics, Mathematics & Computers — 13% — Engineering & Architecture

Technion – Israel Institute of Technology (est. 1924, Haifa) has graduated a high proportion of the country's engineers, architects and town planners. In recent decades, faculties for medicine and the life sciences were added. The Technion serves as a center of basic and applied research in the sciences and engineering to advance the country's industrial development.

The Hebrew University of Jerusalem (est. 1925) comprises faculties which cover nearly all areas of scholarship, from art history to zoology, and houses Israel's National Library. Since its inception, Hebrew University scientists have been actively involved in every phase of Israel's national development, and its Jewish studies departments rank among the most comprehensive in the world.

Weizmann Institute of Science (est. 1934, Rehovot), originally founded as the Sieff Institute, was expanded in 1949 and named for Dr. Chaim Weizmann, Israel's first president and a renowned chemist. Today, it is a recognized post-graduate center of research in physics, chemistry, mathematics and the life sciences. Its researchers are engaged in projects designed to accelerate the development of industry and the establishment of new science-based enterprises. The Institute includes a department for science teaching which prepares curricula for use in high schools.

Bar Ilan University (est. 1955, Ramat Gan) embodies a unique integrative approach which combines enrichment programs in Jewish heritage with a liberal education, in a wide range of disciplines, particularly in the social sciences. Blending tradition with modern technologies, it houses research institutes in physics, medicinal chemistry, mathematics, economics, strategic studies, developmental psychology, musicology, Bible, Talmud, Jewish law and more.

Tel Aviv University (est. 1956) was founded by incorporating three existing institutions to meet the need for a university in the Tel Aviv area, the country's most populous region. Today it is Israel's largest university, offering a wide spectrum of disciplines and placing considerable emphasis on both basic and applied research. The university houses specialized institutes which focus on strategic studies, health systems management, technological forecasting and energy studies.

Haifa University (est. 1963), which serves as a center of higher education in the northern part of the country, offers opportunities for interdisciplinary studies; its interdepartmental centers, institutes and overall architectural plan are structured to facilitate this approach. The university includes a unit for the study of the kibbutz as a social and economic entity, as well as a center dedicated to the advancement of understanding and cooperation between Jews and Arabs in Israel.

Ben-Gurion University of the Negev (est. 1967, Be'er Sheva) was established to serve the residents of southern Israel and to encourage the social and scientific development of the country's desert region. It has made major contributions in arid zone research, and its medical school has pioneered community-oriented medicine in the country. The university's campus at Kibbutz Sde Boker houses a research center for the study of the historical and political aspects of the life and times of David Ben-Gurion, Israel's first prime minister.

COLLEGES

Regional colleges offer academic courses under the auspices of one of the universities, making it possible for students to begin studying for a degree near their home and complete it at the university's main campus.

Some specialized institutes provide various disciplines in art, music, dance, fashion, nursing, rehabilitation therapies, teaching and sports, respectively. Several private degree-granting colleges offer subjects in great demand such as business administration, law, computers, economics and related topics. At some, additional tracks are available, leading to certificates or vocational diplomas in a variety of subjects ranging from technology and agriculture to marketing and hotel trades.

The Open University (est. 1974), patterned on the British model, offers distinctive, non-traditional higher education opportunities towards a bachelor's degree by utilizing flexible methods based primarily on self-study textbooks and guides, supplemented by structured assignments and periodic tutorials, with final examinations.

ADULT EDUCATION

The rapid expansion of opportunities for adult education reflects the challenges facing the education system and the society at large. A wide range of courses sponsored by the Ministry of Education, as well as by public and private institutions, address individual needs ranging from learning the Hebrew language and upgrading basic educational skills to promoting family well-being and expanding general knowledge, while the Ministry of Labor provides vocational training and retraining for adults in many fields. Most programs are available in the large cities, as well as in many towns. All in all, adult education as a leisure activity is becoming increasingly popular in Israel, especially among senior citizens.

Hebrew language instruction on many levels, using the specially-developed ulpan method, helps immigrants and other population groups to integrate into the mainstream of Israeli life. Compensatory education, designed to reduce educational and cultural disparities among adults in Israel, is tailored to the world of adult learners to enable them to complete their formal education. Vocational training courses, both in day and night classes, are available at centers jointly operated by the Ministry of Labor and industrial enterprises, as well as in institutions for technological and professional training. The courses, lasting from a few weeks to one year, include basic instruction, in-service and on-the-job-training, as well as the retraining of academically and professionally trained adults (mainly immigrants) whose professions are not in demand. Family instruction and guidance programs aim at improving the quality of family and community life by developing and enhancing family well-being. 'Popular universities' all over the country offer hundreds of adult education classes and workshops in academic subjects as well as the arts. Special radio broadcasts for immigrants include a 'university on the air' program.

SPORTS

Soccer, basketball, swimming, tennis, volleyball, track-and-field, gymnastics, sailing, weightlifting, judo and fencing are among the most popular sports, with horseback riding, snorkeling, deep sea diving, wind surfing, ice skating, rapelling, cycling and hang gliding rapidly gaining enthusiasts. League soccer, basketball, softball, rugby, cricket and volleyball teams, organized at local, regional and national levels, play a full schedule of games before crowds of loyal fans, with championship events engendering countrywide excitement. Tennis tournaments and swimming meets also draw many spectators. Mass sporting events are very popular. Thousands of Israelis and visitors from abroad take part annually in the Jerusalem March, the swim across Lake Kinneret (Sea of Galilee) and various marathons.

While physical education classes in schools introduce youngsters to sports activities, clubs for teenagers, sponsored by the country's various sports organizations and supported by the Ministry of Education, are the training ground for Israel's future athletes. Sports facilities are provided by regional and local authorities as well as by private centers.

The four major sports organizations are Maccabi (est. 1912), Betar (est. 1924), Hapoel (est. 1923) and Elizur (est. 1939). Jewish athletes from around the world compete in

the Maccabiah Games, known as the 'Jewish Olympics,' held in Israel every four years since 1932. Hapoel stages its own international competition at similar intervals.

Israel belongs to the Asian Games Federation and to Asian sports associations, except for basketball, volleyball and soccer, where the link is with Europe. The Maccabi Tel Aviv basketball team established its place in the world of sports by twice winning the European Cup championship, in 1977 and 1981. Individual players and teams also take part in various international competitions.

Israel has regularly participated in the Olympic Games since 1952. Tragedy struck its team at the 1972 Munich Games, when 11 of its sportsmen were murdered by PLO terrorists. In the 1992 Barcelona Games, Israel won its first medals, in judo.

The Sports Authority of the Ministry of Education, Culture and Sport assists in developing programs, sponsors the training of instructors and coaches at the Wingate Institute of Physical Education, and coordinates the activities of various sports federations and organizations. Proceeds from the national lottery are used to finance a large portion of sports activities and facilities, and to provide annual prizes for outstanding sports achievements.

Educational Television (ETV), a unit of the Ministry of Education, Culture and Sport, produces and boadcasts scholastic programs for use in school classrooms and educational/cultural programs for the entire population. In addition, ETV collaborates with education professionals at universities and teachers' seminars in developing new teaching methods. Dedicated to providing 'lifetime learning,' ETV gears its productions to people of all ages through enrichment programs for preschoolers, entertainment programs for youth, educational courses for adults and news broadcasts for all. ETV is aired on two channels, six days a week, for a total of some ten hours daily.

science and technology

SCIENCE AND TECHNOLOGY

Beginnings

Professional Personnel

Research and Development (R&D)

Worldwide Ties

המחקר המדעי והישגיו אינם עוד עניין
אינטלקטואלי מופשט בלבד... אלא גורם
מרכזי... בחיי עם תרבותי ...
(דוד בן-גוריון, תשכ"ב)

■

Scientific research and its achievements are no longer merely an
abstract intellectual pursuit... but a
central factor... in the life of every
civilized people...
(David Ben-Gurion, 1962)

Israel is a small country in the big world of science and technology. Like many other small countries, it has sharply defined policies towards scientific and technological activities aimed at enhancing its competitive position. In science, Israel encourages the establishment of centers of excellence around outstanding scientists and in areas of vital concern to the development of the industrial sector, while endeavoring to maintain a minimal international level of quality achievement across the broad spectrum of scientific fields. International cooperation continues to play a major role by facilitating the extension of scientific resources and expert knowledge at Israel's disposal. In technology, Israel strives for high performance mainly through specialization, concentrating national efforts on a limited number of areas. The percentage of Israel's population engaged in scientific and technological inquiry as well as the amount spent on research and development (R&D), in relation to the size of its Gross Domestic Product (GDP), are among the highest in the world; and, relative to the size of the labor force, Israel has the largest number of publishing authors in the natural sciences, engineering, agriculture and medicine.

BEGINNINGS

The history of scientific research in Israel is an integral part of the story of the return of the Jewish people to its homeland. Theodor Herzl (1860-1904), the founder of political Zionism and the first to actively promote the idea of a modern Jewish state in the Land of Israel, envisaged it not only as the physical home of the Jewish people but also as a major spiritual, cultural and scientific center.

The desire to transform the Land, then a barren and disease-ridden region, into a modern state was a key factor in subsequent scientific inquiry and technological development. Agricultural research dates back to the end of the 19th century with the establishment of the Mikveh Israel School (1870). The Agricultural Station, set up in Tel Aviv (1921), eventually became the Agricultural Research Organization (ARO), today Israel's major institution of agricultural research and development. Medical and public health research was initiated prior to World War I with the founding of the Hebrew Health Station. It received a major boost when the Institute of Microbiology and departments of biochemistry, bacteriology and hygiene were instituted (mid-1920s) at the Hebrew University of Jerusalem, which provided the basis for the Hadassah Medical Center, today Israel's most prominent medical research facility. Industrial research was pioneered at the Dead Sea Laboratories in the 1930s, and advances in basic science and technology were begun at the Hebrew University (est. 1925), the Technion-Israel Institute of Technology (est. 1924 in Haifa) and the Daniel Sieff Research Center (est. 1934 in Rehovot), which later became the Weizmann Institute of Science (1949).

When the State of Israel was established (1948), the country's scientific and technological infrastructure was already in place, facilitating further advancement. At first, research focused on projects of national importance, and on this foundation commercially-oriented industries gradually developed.

PROFESSIONAL PERSONNEL

Israel's large reservoir of qualified personnel is primarily responsible for its scientific and technological attainments. In 1994 university graduates comprised 19 percent of the country's workers. As the many highly-trained scientists, engineers and technicians among the hundreds of thousands of immigrants from the former Soviet Union gradually enter the labor force, this percentage is rising dramatically and will significantly affect Israel's scientific and technological achievements for decades to come.

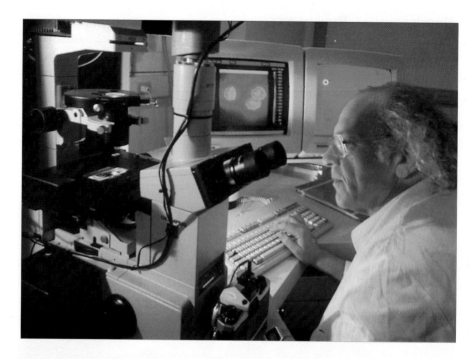

RESEARCH AND DEVELOPMENT (R&D)

R&D in Israel is carried out primarily at seven universities, dozens of government and public research institutes and hundreds of civilian and military enterprises. Significant research is also performed at medical centers and by a number of public service firms, in fields such as telecommunications, electricity and power production and water resources management.

Government and public bodies are primary sources of R&D funding, providing financial support for well over half of Israel's R&D activities. The major share of these funds for civilian R&D purposes is allocated for economic development, mainly in industrial and agricultural spheres, which, in comparison to other countries, constitutes a very large part of the total; over 40 percent is earmarked for advancement of knowledge through national, binational and government research funds as well as through the General University Funds, provided by the Planning and Budgeting Committee of the Council of Higher Education; and the remainder is dedicated to various health and social welfare fields.

R&D AT UNIVERSITIES

As at universities all over the world, advancement of basic scientific knowledge is the chief objective of researchers at Israel's universities. Publications of books and articles by Israelis, encompassing all scientific fields, are a primary expression of the university sector's output; their number, relative to total world publications, is increasing, and they have a high professional impact in the world scientific community as measured by average citations per article. Relative to the size of its labor force, Israel has a significantly larger number of publishing authors in the natural sciences, engineering, agriculture and medicine than any other country, and a higher share of the country's publications are co-authored by Israeli scientists and those of other countries than is the case elsewhere.

To integrate Israeli science into the international scientific community, post-doctoral research positions and sabbaticals abroad as well as attendance at foreign scientific conferences are encouraged, and a wide range of exchange programs and joint projects are maintained at institute, university and government levels with counterpart organizations overseas. Israel is also an important center for international scientific conferences, hosting over 100 such gatherings annually.

Concomitant with their scientific research activities, the universities continue to play an important and innovative role in Israel's technological advancement. The Weizmann Institute of Science was among the first in the world to set up an organization for the commercial utilization of its research (1958); today similar organizations exist at all Israeli universities. The establishment of science-based industrial parks adjacent to university campuses has been pioneered with

---

The number of **patents** taken out by Israel's universities is one measure of the effectiveness of the relationship between the universities and industry. A recent study has shown that the universities are the country's leading patentees both at home and abroad, and that the relative size of their patenting activity far exceeds that of higher education sectors in other countries. Furthermore, in relation to their expenditures on R&D, Israel's universities were granted more than twice as many patents as American universities and nine times more than those in Canada.

---

great commercial success. Universities have also set up 'spin-off' industrial firms for the commercialization of specific products based on their research, often in partnership with local and foreign concerns.

Interdisciplinary research and testing institutes are functioning at universities in diverse scientific and technological fields vital to the country's industry, serving areas such as construction, transportation and education as national focal points for applied R&D. In addition, a high proportion of faculty serve industry in an advisory capacity on technical, administrative, financial and managerial matters. The universities' share of research grants and contracts funded by local industry is over 9 percent, as compared with 6-7 percent in the United States and Canada.

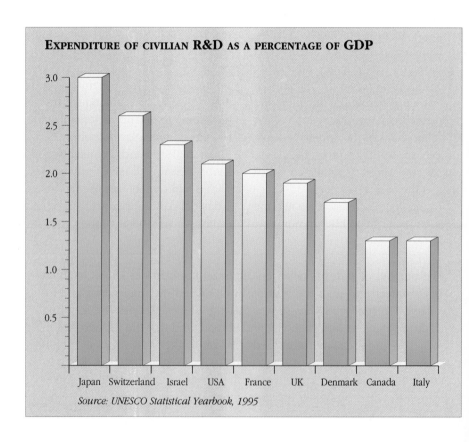

EXPENDITURE OF CIVILIAN **R&D** AS A PERCENTAGE OF **GDP**

Source: UNESCO Statistical Yearbook, 1995

MEDICAL R&D

Israel has made significant theoretical and practical contributions to the biotechnology revolution and has developed an advanced infrastructure of medical and paramedical research as well as bioengineering capabilities. Clinical medicine and biomedical research account for over half of all scientific publications. The country's industrial sector has increased its activities in the medical field to capitalize on its extensive knowledge base.

Local scientists have developed methods for producing a human growth hormone and interferon, a group of proteins effective against viral infections. Genetic engineering, including cloning, has resulted in a wide range of diagnostic kits based on monoclonal antibodies, along with other microbiological products.

Sophisticated medical equipment for both diagnostic and treatment purposes has been developed and marketed worldwide such as computer tomography (CT) scanners, magnetic resonance imaging (MRI) systems, ultrasound scanners, nuclear medical cameras and surgical lasers. Other innovations include a controlled-release liquid polymer to prevent accumulation of tooth plaque; a device to reduce both benign and malignant swellings of the prostate gland; the use of botulin to correct eye squint.

Industrial R&D

In the rapidly growing industrial sector, civilian industrial R&D expenditures increased more than 13-fold between 1969 and 1985, while the number of scientists and engineers engaged in R&D increased almost 5-fold. Israel's industrial R&D is characterized by a high concentration in electronics (67 percent) as well as by the fact that most activities are carried out in a small number of large firms. Studies have shown that R&D-intensive companies have been the major source of growth of industrial employment and exports over the years.

Fostering the continued growth of such enterprises, both large and small, is the focus of Israel's industrial strategy. The government promotes R&D in industry within the framework of the Law for the Encouragement of Research and Development, implemented by the Chief Scientist's Office of the Ministry of Trade and Industry, which in 1994 alone funded some 1,270 projects in 800 companies. R&D-related products are estimated today to comprise more than one half of total industrial exports (excluding diamonds).

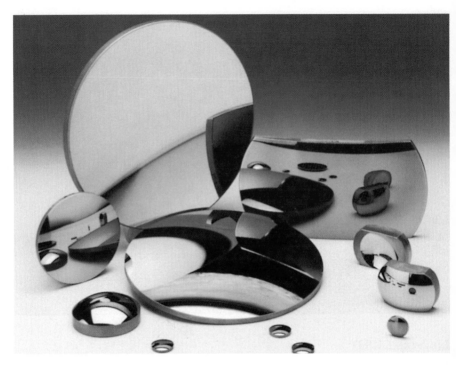

Electronics, limited until the late 1960s mainly to consumer goods, has branched out into more sophisticated technological developments, both military and civilian. In communications, R&D-based applications include the digitalizing, processing, transmitting and enhancing of images, speech and data. Products range from advanced telephone exchanges to voice messaging systems and telephone line doublers.

Optics, electro-optics and lasers as industrial fields have been growing rapidly. Israel is a world leader in fiber-optics, electro-optic inspection systems for printed circuit boards, thermal imaging night-vision systems and electro-optics-based robotic manufacturing systems.

Computer-based equipment, mostly in software and peripheral fields, has been developed and produced. In printing and publishing, Israeli-made computer graphics and computer-based imaging systems are being widely used locally and abroad. Educational activities in schools are enhanced by a variety of computer-aided instructional systems, many of which have been developed for export. While some of Israel's software products are designed for use on mainframe computers, most have been developed for small or medium-sized systems such as computer workstations.

Robotics, first researched in the late 1970s, is now producing robots designed to perform a wide variety of tasks, including diamond polishing, welding, packing, building and other industrial functions. Research is now underway in the application of artificial intelligence to robots.

Aeronautics related to defense needs have generated technological development with consequent civilian spin-offs. The Arava, the first civilian aircraft to be produced in Israel, was followed by the Westwind executive jet. Recently, locally designed and manufactured satellites have been produced and launched by Israel Aircraft Industries in cooperation with the Israel Space Agency. In addition, Israel develops, manufactures and exports a large number of related items, including display systems, aeronautical computers, instrumentation systems and flight simulators, and is a world leader in technology and production of drones.

Amos *communications satellite, control room, 1996*

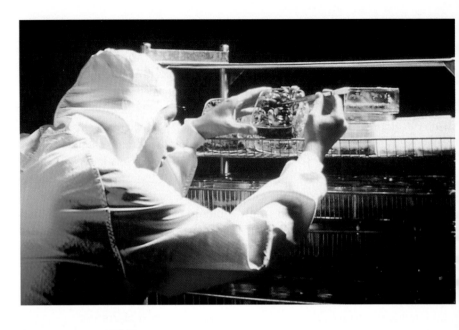

Agricultural R&D

The agricultural sector is based almost entirely on R&D, implemented by cooperation between farmers and researchers. Research results are quickly transmitted through an extension service system to the field for trial, and problems are brought directly to the scientists for solutions. Agricultural R&D is carried out primarily by the Ministry of Agriculture's Agricultural Research Organization. Most agricultural research institutes in Israel maintain close relations with the Food and Agriculture Organization of the United Nations, ensuring a continuous exchange of information with other countries.

Israel's dairy cows are, on average, the world champions in milk production, having increased the average yield per cow from 6,300 liters in 1970 to 10,000 liters today through scientific breeding and genetic testing carried out by the Volcani Institute. By harvesting sperm and ova from cattle of superior bloodlines, Israel is able to upgrade its own herd as well as share its advances in this field with other countries.

Israeli agriculturists have pioneered agricultural biotechnology, trickle-drip irrigation, soil solarization and the sustained use of industrial waste water for agriculture. These advances have been applied to marketable products, ranging from genetically-engineered seeds and biopesticides to light-degradable plastics and computerized irrigation/fertilization systems.

Making optimal use of scarce water, harsh land and a limited labor force has led to revolutions in agricultural methods. The search for water-saving techniques spurred development of computer-controlled irrigation systems, including the drip method which directs water flow straight to the root zone of plants. As the result of intensive research, the huge underground reservoir of brackish water under the Negev is now being exploited to produce crops such as prime-quality tomatoes for European and American winter markets. Research relating to the electromagnetic treatment of water to improve animal health and crop yields is also producing promising results.

Israeli-designed and manufactured computers are widely used to coordinate daily farming activities such as guiding fertilizer injection while monitoring relevant environmental factors; supplying feed for livestock mixed according to tested least-cost/best-yield proportions; and providing a temperature and humidity controlled environment for poultry. In addition, a variety of innovative equipment for tilling, sowing, planting, harvesting, collecting, sorting and packing has been developed, manufactured and implemented.

Agriculture has also benefited from general scientific research and R&D developments, including automated plant tissue culture, biological insecticides, disease-resistant seeds and biological fertilization.

ENERGY R&D

Extensive development of alternative energy sources such as solar, thermal and wind energy has been a positive outcome of the country's lack of conventional energy sources. As a result, Israel is a leader in the solar energy field at every level and the world's largest per capita user of solar water heaters in the home. Recently a new, high-efficiency receiver to collect concentrated sunlight has been developed which will enhance the use of solar energy in industry as well.

An advance in harnessing wind energy has been the production of a wind turbine with a flexible, inflatable rotor. Technology utilizing pond water with a certain degree of salinity and mineral composition to absorb and store solar energy has been developed. Geothermal power stations, capable of extracting heat from the ground and converting it to steam for powering turbines, are now being tested. A newly-approved project, developed by a team of scientists at the Technion, uses dry air and water (even sea or brackish water) to produce energy through 1,000-meter high chimneys.

WORLDWIDE TIES

Israel's international relations, a dynamic and substantive feature of its scientific and development activities, are maintained at all levels, from various national frameworks to the individual researcher. Vital to the advancement of the country's R&D has been the establishment of several binational research foundations involved in activities, ranging from basic research to industrial development and marketing.

US-Israel Binational Science Foundation (BSF), set up (1974) to foster civilian research, is financed in equal proportion by the two countries. Its present endowment totals $100 million. BSF funds basic and applied research projects in many fields, ranging from anthropology and biomedical engineering to physics and environmental sciences. Since its inception, BSF has awarded nearly 2,000 grants at an expenditure of over $90 million.

US-Israel Binational Agricultural Research and Development Fund (BARD) was established (1977) to promote and support agricultural R&D for the mutual benefit of both countries. Joint research proposals are submitted by at least one cooperating investigator from each country. BARD's income, from which it allocates financing for new projects, derives from an endowment established by the two countries, which at present totals some $110 million.

US-Israel Binational Industrial Research and Development Foundation (BIRD-F), the first arrangement of its kind between the United States and another country, was established (1977) to stimulate cooperation between high-tech industries by supporting all aspects of R&D through which an innovation becomes a commercial product, including product engineering and test marketing. All projects must be proposed jointly by firms from both countries and must be of prospective benefit to both. To date, BIRD-F has approved over 200 projects in telecommunications, electronics, computer software/hardware and medical equipment, leading to sales that recently topped $1 billion. It is funded by an endowment to which both countries contributed equally, worth today some $110 million.

German-Israel Foundation for Scientific Research and Development (GIF) was set up (1987) to support basic and applied research in areas of mutual interest. Its capital comes in equal shares from the two countries and has reached DM150 million. GIF supports selected joint research projects in such fields as the life sciences, medicine, chemistry, physics, mathematics, technology, agriculture and the social sciences.

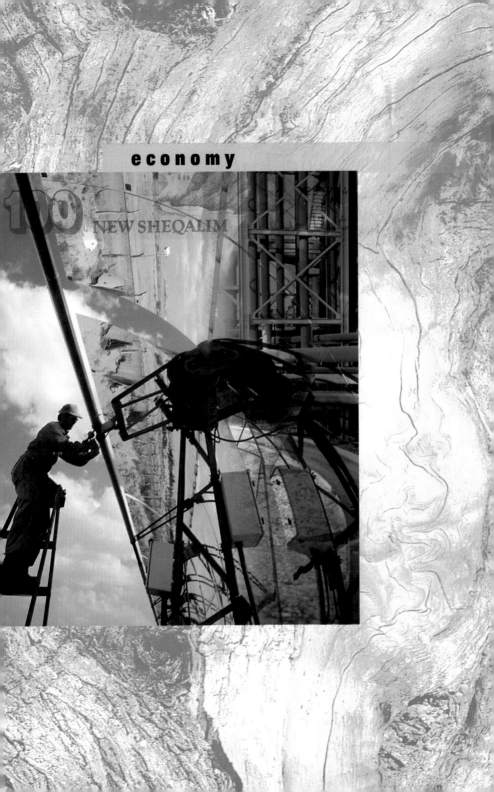

economy

100 NEW SHEQALIM

ECONOMY

FOUR CHALLENGES
BALANCE OF PAYMENTS
AN ECONOMIC PICTURE
ECONOMIC SECTORS

עובד אדמתו ישבע לחם...
(משלי י"ב: י"א)

■

He who tills the land shall be
satisfied with bread...
(Proverbs 12:11)

Israel has attained the highest Gross Domestic Product (GDP) growth rate among Western (OECD) economies during the 1990s, averaging 5.6 percent in 1990-93 and 6.8 percent in 1994-95. Its per capita GDP, today exceeding $16,000 ($=US dollar), places it 21st among 200 countries in the world. Although a small country (population over 5.5 million), Israel's international position in some areas of industrial and agricultural production capacity and exports is remarkable. Free trade agreements with Europe (the European Union and European Free Trade Association) and the United States facilitate Israel's $18 billion of exports and its participation in international business enterprises, contributing to the country's accelerated growth since 1990.

FOUR CHALLENGES

Israel's most striking economic achievement is the rate at which it has developed while simultaneously dealing with a number of enormously expensive challenges:

Maintaining national security: Israel now spends some ten percent (as against over 25 percent in the 1970s) of its GDP on defense. Even in an era of peace Israel must retain a strong deterrent capability.

Absorbing large numbers of immigrants: The 'ingathering of the exiles' is the *raison d'être* of the Jewish state. Since its inception, Israel has absorbed over 2.5 million immigrants, nearly four times the number of Jews living in the country when it attained independence (1948). In its first four years alone, Israel's population more than doubled as 700,000 immigrants, mostly refugees from postwar Europe and the Arab states,

poured into the country. In the 1990s another wave of immigrants (about 700,000, mainly from the former Soviet Union), is accelerating GDP growth, although it increased unemployment to an 11.2 percent high in 1992, which was brought down to 6.3 percent by 1995.

Establishing a modern economic infrastructure: Although basic networks of roads, transportation and port facilities, water, electricity and communications existed in 1948, they were far from adequate, requiring enormous outlays for their development and expansion.

Providing a high level of public services: As Israel is committed to ensuring the well-being of its population, with special concern for the weaker elements in the society, much of its resources has always been used to meet these obligations.

An industrial park

'AN ECONOMIC MIRACLE'

For the first 25 years, the economy reached a striking average growth rate in the GDP of about 10 percent annually, while at the same time absorbing several mass immigrations, building a modern economy, fighting four wars and maintaining security. This 'economic miracle' is ascribed largely to the use made of economic aid received over the years, enabling mass capital investment in means of production, and to the country's success in rapidly absorbing immigrants and involving them in productive settings. Between 1973 and 1979 the growth rate decreased (as in most industrialized countries, partly due to the oil crises of 1973/4 and 1979/80) to a yearly average of 3.8 percent and, in the 1980s, it dwindled to 3.1 percent. Since 1990 it has averaged 6 percent. In 1995 the total GDP was approximately $90 billion ($16,260 per capita), a 24-fold real increase since 1950.

THE BALANCE OF PAYMENTS

The perennial problem of the trade deficit is the difficult price Israel has to pay for the 'miracle' of attaining rapid growth while successfully meeting the four national challenges. This yearly gap between a high level of imports and a significantly smaller scale of exports indicates economic dependence on foreign resources. Thus, a primary policy goal of every Israeli government has been to achieve economic independence, the point where exports will finance all imports.

However, the deficit has continuously grown, from $280 million in 1950 to $11.1 billion in 1995. Nevertheless, the burden of the deficit is actually decreasing in relative terms, indicating that the problem is gradually being solved: Whereas in 1950 exports financed only 14 percent of imports, in 1960 this ratio grew to 51 percent, and in 1995 it stood at 73 percent. This improvement and the decline in the external debt have stopped recently owing to accelerated imports to facilitate the GDP's surge and a reduction in unemployment.

BALANCE OF TRADE*: 1949-1995
(in millions of current US dollars)

Year	Imports	Exports	Deficit
1949	263	43	220
1955	443	139	304
1960	694	352	342
1970	2,657	1,374	1,283
1975	8,038	4,022	4,016
1980	13,832	10,099	3,733
1985	15,138	11,223	3,915
1990	24,217	18,868	5,349
1995	40,472	29,652	11,090

* *in goods and services*

NET EXTERNAL DEBT: 1954-1995*
(in millions of current US dollars)

Year	Total Net External Debt
1954	356
1960	543
1970	2,223
1975	6,286
1980	11,344
1985	18,051
1990	15,122
1995	19,217

* Total liabilities minus total foreign assets

Over and above what the economy has managed to produce itself, the total amount of aid which it required during Israel's first half a century to cover the annual trade deficits is $111 billion (in current figures). Nearly two thirds of this sum was provided by unilateral transfers such as funds brought in by immigrants, foreign pensions, donations from Jewish fund-raising organizations abroad to social service, health and educational institutions, and foreign government grants, especially from the United States. The rest was financed by loans from individuals, banks and foreign governments, which Israel has been repaying since its first years. The external debt increased every year until 1985, when, for the first time, and since (excepting 1991), less was borrowed than paid back. The bulk of this debt is governmental (owed to the United States) and for a very long term.

FOREIGN TRADE

A small economy with a relatively limited domestic market, Israel can only boost growth by expanding exports. Much of the country's creative resources have been devoted to building up its industrial exports, which have grown over 1300 times (in current prices) over 45 years, from $13 million in 1950 to $52 million in 1955 to $1.4 billion in 1975 to $5.6 billion in 1985 and to $16.95 billion in 1995. In recent years, about 70 percent of all imports of goods have been production inputs and fuel. In 1995, 46 percent of all exports of goods were directed to Europe, 32 percent to the Americas, 12 percent to Asia, and 9 percent to other countries.

The competitiveness of Israel's exports has been enhanced by its joining the General Agreement of Tariffs and Trade (GATT), as well as by instituting a free trade area for industrial products with the European Community (1975) and for all products with the United States (1985). Thus Israeli goods can enter duty free both the European Union (EU) and the United States (together comprising 630 million consumers), enabling local producers to aim for a market over a hundred times wider than the domestic one and attracting investors to Israel who wish to export their products to Europe without paying duty. To maximize chances for success, local enterprises have sought to identify segments of international trade where they can carve out specialized niches for themselves. The establishment of joint ventures with foreign industrial firms has often utilized the strength of the Israeli company in innovation and those of the foreign firm in large-scale production and market penetration. Joint projects have been undertaken in areas such as electronics, software, medical equipment, printing and computerized graphics, with many actively assisted by binational frameworks such as the Israel-US Binational Industrial and Development Research Foundation (BIRD-F), which is supported by both governments and acts as a capital foundation for joint American-Israeli ventures.

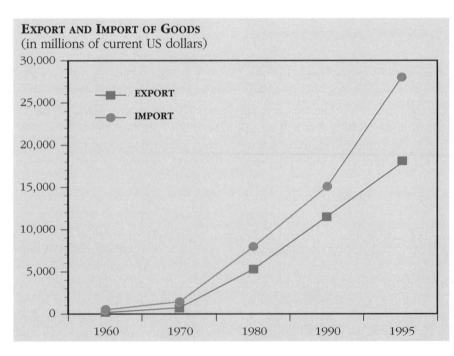

EXPORT AND IMPORT OF GOODS
(in millions of current US dollars)

The **shekel,** Israel's unit of currency, (valued at $0.33 in 1995), was known as early as the second millennium BCE as a unit of weight for means of payment in gold and silver. It is recorded in the Bible that Abraham negotiated the purchase of a field *"and the cave that was therein,"* at Machpela (near Hebron), saying: *"I will give thee money for the field; take it of me, and I will bury my dead there."* Ephron, the landowner, replied: *"The land is worth four hundred shekels of silver...and Abraham weighed to Ephron... four hundred shekels of silver, current money with the merchant"* (Genesis 23:13, 15-17).

AN ECONOMIC PICTURE
CHECKING INFLATION

The economy has always suffered from rising prices, but a linkage mechanism left individuals virtually untouched by their consequences. All financial commitments, salaries, rents, savings accounts, life insurance policies, income tax brackets and the like were linked to a steadier value (such as foreign currency rates or the consumer price index), thereby taking the sting out of inflation. Thus, whether the annual inflation rate was one digit (mid-1950s to the end of the 1960s), two digits (1970s) or three digits (early 1980s), Israelis still managed to raise their standard of living.

Obviously, the economy at large suffered from the inflation (e.g. decline in investments), much of which was fueled by this linkage, until the situation blew up in the mid-1980s.

In the summer of 1985, after inflation had soared from 191 percent in 1983 to 445 percent in 1984 and threatened to reach four digits in 1985, the government implemented a radical emergency stabilization program. The inflation rate fell to 185 percent in 1985, ranged between 16 and 20 percent between 1986 and 1991, and fell further to 8 percent in 1995.

THE PUBLIC SECTOR

The high level of public consumption, mostly the weight of the government's budget deficit, has always been a primary cause of Israel's high inflation rate. All the resources the government can recruit to finance the budget (domestic and foreign sources, loans by the public, direct and indirect taxes) have been insufficient to cover the amount spent, and the government has found itself repeatedly compelled to resort to inflationary financing.

The path to economic recovery by cutting inflation, reducing the balance-of-payments deficit and maintaining the rapid economic growth rate requires decreasing public consumption ($25.3 billion in 1995). The high ratio of public consumption to the GNP, brought down from 41 to 28 percent from 1980 to 1995, is due not only to the tremendous defense burden and the need to repay internal and external debts (two items which only in the last few years have contracted from two thirds to one half of the government budget), but also because of the government's still excessive involvement in and encouragement of economic initiatives. Economic policy has, since the mid-1980s, been striving to substantially reduce this involvement in all its forms by almost eliminating subsidies on basic commodities, promoting investments and exports, and selling full or partial ownership of hundreds of public enterprises. Recently, the government initiated a privatization campaign to lower the number of such enterprises as well as to create an additional source of income.

The Tax System

Since financing Israel's massive public consumption has required heavy taxation, in some years the Israeli citizen has borne one of the highest tax burdens, relative to income, in the world. During the first decade of statehood, taxes equaled one eighth of GNP; in the 1960s, the proportion reached one quarter, wavered between 30 and 47 percent in the 1970s and 1980s; in 1990-95 it averaged 40 percent. At no time, however, has taxation covered more than two thirds of the government budget.

Until the late 1970s, indirect taxes (on consumption and expenditures) such as customs duties, excise tax, purchase tax, Value Added Tax (VAT, which stands at 17 percent at present) and the like accounted for the bulk of tax collections.

Direct taxes (on income and property) amounted to less than one quarter of all tax revenues until the late 1950s, climbed to around one third by the early 1970s, to about one half in the early 1980s and reached a high of 55 percent in 1983. Since then the weight of direct taxes decreased to 45 percent in 1992 but stood at nearly 50 percent in 1995, when total state revenues from taxes and fees were some $35.7 billion.

Private Consumption and Savings

Although private consumption has risen almost without a break since 1950, with its growth averaging 3.2 percent annually since 1970 (4.5 percent in 1995), private savings were consistently substantial. Until the late 1950s, the average ratio of private savings to private disposable income never fell below 29 percent; in the early 1960s, it dropped to 21 percent; it rose again in 1972 to 38 percent, fell in the subsequent decade to 34 percent, further still to 29 percent in 1985 and to 22 percent in 1995.

INVESTMENT

The rate of savings, large as it was, has not been sufficient to support the immense investments (generally 20-30 percent of all available resources) made by the rapidly growing economy. Consequently, a large proportion was financed by public and private transfers of capital from abroad as well as directly from the public sector, mainly the government. Gross investment in 1995 totaled approximately $21.6 billion.

Many private investments, of both domestic and foreign origin, were also made as a result of government initiative and encouragement, as reflected over the years in the various versions of the Encouragement of Capital Investment Law. Through this law, the government attracted investors by assisting them with subsidized long-term loans (bearing reduced interest rates), direct grants as a percentage of the total investment and R&D financing, as well as with tax relief and tax rebates, allocated in accordance with the weight of the contribution by the specific investment to the implementation of economic policy such as population dispersion, promotion of exports and the like. This assistance may have accounted for the accumulation during the previous decade of capital stock (production capacity) at a rate exceeding the growth of the GDP. In some sectors, this surplus production capacity has facilitated the rapid take-off in the 1990s.

WAGES AND WORKING CONDITIONS

Wages are determined through negotiations conducted between the government (also the country's largest employer), whose wage scale has strong repercussions on all segments of the economy, the Histadrut (General Federation of Labor) and the organization of private sector employers. The agreements reached constitute a framework of wage scales for the different sectors of the economy and, with occasional changes of detail, also provide for automatic payment of a cost-of-living allowance as compensation for inflation. Thus the wage situation is rather inflexible, especially at the lower end. Waves of unemployment in Israel do not significantly reduce wages, although in times of labor shortages wages rise with greater elasticity in those sectors where the demand for workers is more acute. In 1995 the average monthly wage was NIS 4,614 (about $1,530).

Conditions for workers in the country's various economic sectors are set forth in work agreements negotiated between employers and employees. Minimum requirements, however, are anchored in law and include a maximum 47-hour work week, minimum wages, compensation for overtime, severance payments, paid vacation and sick leave.

Histadrut – New General Federation of Labor was established in 1920 as a federation of trade unions to represent the country's workers and to set up industries to provide jobs for its members. In time, it became one of Israel's largest employers and played an important role in the development of the country. Since 1992, it has been in the process of selling off some of its holdings. Histadrut members comprise most of the country's labor force and include Jews and Arabs representing all economic sectors as well as the free professions. The Histadrut offers its members a variety of social benefits through a network of medical, educational, recreational, welfare and legal services.

Major Indicators by Economic Branch (1995)
(in percent)

Branch	GNP	Labor Force	Exports	Investment
Industry	22	20	61	22
Agriculture	3	4	3	2
Construction	7	10	–	30
Transportation and Communications	8	6	10	27
Commercial, Financial and Personal Services	27	34	26	8
Public Services	33	26	–	11

Source: Bank of Israel, Annual Report, 1995

Economic Sectors

Agriculture

Agriculture in Israel is a success story of a long, hard struggle against adverse conditions and of making maximum use of scarce water and arable land. When Jews began resettling their historic homeland in the late 19th century, their first efforts were directed to turning barren land into fertile fields.

Since Israel attained independence (1948), the total area under cultivation has increased by a factor of 2.6 to approximately 1.1 million acres,

and irrigated land has increased by a factor of 8 to about 0.6 million acres. This growth ceased during the 1980s as a result of an intensifying shortage of water and the urbanization process. During the same period, the number of agricultural settlements has grown from 400 to 750, but, as the society has become less rural, the proportion of the population living in them has fallen from 12 percent to less than 6 percent.

Today Israel meets most of its food needs through domestic production, supplemented by imports, mainly of grain, oilseeds, meat, coffee, cocoa and sugar, which are more than financed by agricultural exports. Its farm production consists largely of diary and poultry products as well as a large variety of flowers, fruit and vegetables. During the winter months, Israel is Europe's greenhouse, exporting long-stemmed roses, spray carnations, melons, tomatoes, cucumbers, peppers, strawberries, kiwis, mangoes, avocados and a wide variety of citrus fruits.

The secret of Israel's agricultural success lies in the close interaction between farmers and government-sponsored researchers, who cooperate in developing and applying sophisticated methods in all agricultural branches, as well as technological advancement, new irrigation techniques and innovative agromechanical equipment.

The share of agricultural production in the GNP declined from 11 percent to 3 percent between 1950 and the 1990s, while the proportion of agricultural exports decreased from 60 percent to 3 percent of total exports, despite an absolute increase of annual exports from $20 million to $740 million (in 1995) due, inter alia, to the widespread introduction of innovative farming methods and export-oriented farming.

INDUSTRY

Today's dynamic, widely diversified industrial sector developed from workshops set up a century ago to manufacture farm implements and process agricultural products. An incentive to local industry was given during World War II (1939-45) when the Allied forces in the region required various commodities, especially clothing and canned foods. However, modern industry attained significant development only in the early 1960s, since in the 1950s most resources were directed towards developing agriculture and constructing a national infrastructure.

In view of the country's highly qualified labor force and a lack of raw materials, industry has concentrated on manufactured products with high added values by developing products based on Israel's own scientific creativity and technological innovation. Until the 1970s, traditional industrial branches such as food processing, textiles and fashion, furniture, fertilizers, pesticides, pharmaceuticals, chemicals, and rubber, plastic and metal products provided most of the country's industrial output. In the past two decades, it has made international-level strides in the fields of medical electronics, agrotechnology, telecommunications, fine chemicals, computer hardware and software, and diamond cutting and polishing. The highest growth rates are in the high-tech sectors which are skill and capital intensive and require sophisticated production techniques as well as considerable investment in R&D.

Israel's diamond industry export exceeded $4.6 billion in 1995, producing about 80 percent of the world output of small polished stones, which comprise most of the gems used in jewelry settings. It is also responsible for 40 percent of the polishing of diamonds of all sizes and shapes, making Israel the world's leading diamond polishing center in terms of both production and marketing.

In 1995, some 19,000 industrial firms employing more than 412,000 workers (14 percent of them with higher education) produced an output of $50 billion, 34 percent of which was exported. Unlike the developed economies in which the number of employed in industry has remained stable or diminished during the 1990s (except Japan which had a 2.4 percent growth), in Israel their number has grown by 16.8 percent.

Israel's 32.5 percent industrial output growth rate during 1990-94 was second highest (Korea's was 34.5 percent) among Western economies. Investments in industry amounted to $4.3 billion in 1995, a 10 percent rise compared to 1994 (when a 24 percent rise was recorded). The most significant growth in industry has occurred in the high-tech sectors, which accounted for 37 percent of the industrial product in 1965, 58 percent in 1985 and 62 percent in recent years. Almost half of the high-tech product is exported (providing 66 percent of total industrial exports), while more traditional, low-tech firms export some 39 percent of their product. Over 90 percent of the $650 million devoted to research and development in industry in 1995 was spent by high-tech firms.

CONSTRUCTION

In the early years of the state, residential building accounted for 84 percent of total construction output. Subsequently, it fluctuated between 70-75 percent until 1991 when it rose to 86 percent to meet renewed immigration. Accordingly, the construction sector output rose sharply in 1990-91. The number of residential units built yearly has fluctuated between 83,000 and 33,000 since, reaching 62,600 in 1995. Once considered a leading economic activity and a barometer of the economy, the construction sector in 1995 contributed only 6.5 percent to the GNP, down from 30 percent in 1950.

While at first almost all construction was the result of government initiative and investment, between 1958 and 1989 its share fell gradually, from 67 to 16 percent. However, it rose again (to 74 percent in 1991) when the private sector could not meet the demand created by the sudden influx of hundreds of thousands of immigrants. The government's share stood at 44 percent in 1995.

TRANSPORT AND COMMUNICATIONS

Contributing approximately 8 percent of GNP, the transport and communications sector constitutes some 10 percent of exports of goods and services and employs 6 percent of the country's labor force. Forty-seven percent of its product is in land transportation, 22 percent in shipping and aviation, 20 percent in communications and the rest in various services, including storage and parking. Since the early 1950s the total gross tonnage of the merchant fleet has grown more than 10-fold, while air carriers now fly more than 100 times as many passengers. During the same period, road length was doubled, the number of transport buses more than tripled and the number of trucks increased 10-fold.

TOURISM

In 1995, some 2.53 million people visited the country, compared to 33,000 in 1950, 118,000 in 1960, 441,000 in 1970, 1.18 million in 1980, and 1.34 million in 1990. Attracted by Israel's geographical diversity, archaeological and religious sites, almost unlimited sunshine and modern resort facilities on the Mediterranean, Lake Kinneret (Sea of Galilee), the Red Sea and the Dead Sea, nearly 90 percent of the annual influx comes from Europe and the Americas, while others come from the world over, including visitors from Arab lands.

Tourism is a major source of foreign currency earnings ($3.1 billion in

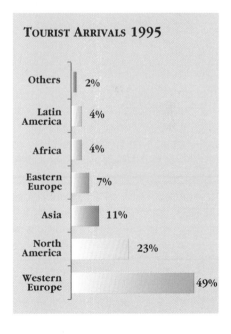

TOURIST ARRIVALS 1995

Others	2%
Latin America	4%
Africa	4%
Eastern Europe	7%
Asia	11%
North America	23%
Western Europe	49%

1995), contributing 3.5 percent to the GNP and 10.6 percent of total exports, with an added value of 85 percent (making it the added-value leader among the country's export industries). Some 50,000 employees are directly involved in tourism infrastructure. Tourism, with its enormous potential, is a major factor in Israel's economic plans to eliminate the deficit in its balance of payments.

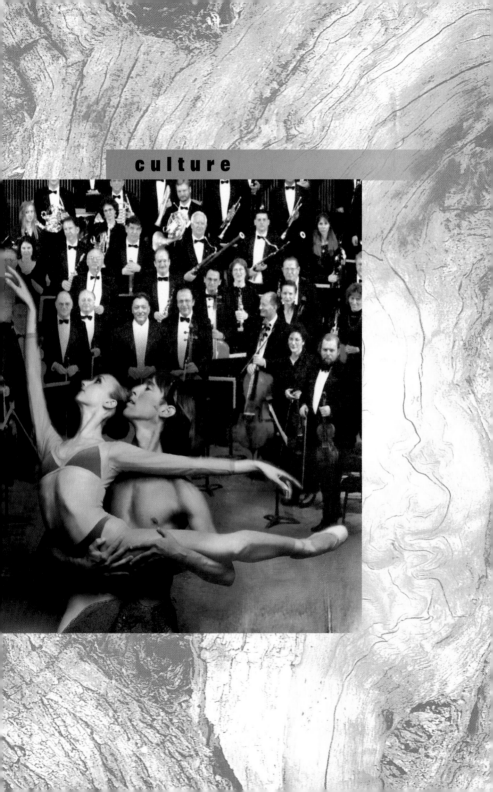

culture

CULTURE

LITERATURE

FINE ARTS

MUSEUMS

MUSIC

DANCE

THEATER

CINEMA

LIGHT ENTERTAINMENT

MEDIA

...כי לא על הלחם לבדו יחיה האדם...
(דברים ח': ג')

■

...Know that man does not live
by bread alone...
(Deuteronomy 8:3)

Marc Chagall: *The Twelve Tribes*

Israel is an old-new country, small in size, but with a widely varied landscape and a culturally active, heterogeneous population of over 5.5 million. It is a place where East meets West, where past and present touch, and where ideologies mold lifestyles. Four thousand years of Jewish heritage, more than a century of Zionism, the 'ingathering of the exiles' and nearly five decades of modern statehood have contributed to a culture which has already created an identity of its own, while preserving the uniqueness of 70 different communities. Emerging from the encounter between the individual and the society, it blends tradition and innovation, and strives to steer a course between Israeli particularism and universalism.

A largely immigrant and second-generation society, Israel's creative expression has absorbed many different cultural and social influences, as the traditions of each group not only vie with those of other groups, but also contend with the country's recent history and life in a Middle Eastern context. The constant search for cultural identity is expressed through creativity in a broad range of art forms, appreciated and enjoyed by a great many people as part of daily life.

LITERATURE

Israel is a source of inspiration for the country's writers and poets. A developing nation built on an ancient heritage, it exists in the midst of complex social relationships. Changes have occurred swiftly and sharply, as witnessed by the pioneering period, the struggle for independence, state building, wars and mass immigrations from many parts of the world. Every new era, every social change has brought new challenges, creating a dynamic of constant restlessness. Each of these alone and all combined provide material for creative writing. Prose and poetry draw motifs, images and a wealth of expression from the Bible, other Jewish sources (such as *Mishna, Talmud* and *Kabbala*) and the creative traditions of the Jewish people in the Diaspora, as well as from the language and cadences of daily speech.

REVIVAL OF THE HEBREW LANGUAGE

Hebrew is the language of Israel. Although it virtually ceased to be spoken around 200 CE, it continued to be used by Jews throughout the ages as the 'sacred tongue' in liturgy, philosophy and literature. In the late 19th century, it emerged as a modern cultural medium, becoming a vital factor in the national revival movement which culminated in political Zionism. The British Mandate administration recognized Hebrew as an official language, together with English and Arabic, and its use was adopted by Jewish institutions and their educational networks. Hebrew press and literature flourished with new generations of authors and readers, and today it is a rich, vibrant, living tongue. From some 8,000 words in biblical times, Hebrew vocabulary has expanded to more than 120,000 words. Its formal linguistic development is guided by the Academy of the Hebrew Language (est. 1953).

Eliezer Ben-Yehuda (1858-1922) spearheaded the momentum for the revival of Hebrew as a spoken language. After immigrating to the Land of Israel in 1881, he pioneered Hebrew usage in home and school, coined thousands of new words, established two Hebrew language periodicals, co-initiated the Hebrew Language Committee (1890) and compiled several volumes of a 17-volume Complete Dictionary of Ancient and Modern Hebrew, which was begun in 1910 and completed by his second wife and son in 1959.

PROSE

Modern Hebrew prose in the Land of Israel was first written by immigrant authors. Althought their roots were anchored in the world and traditions of East European Jewry, their works dealt primarily with the creative achievements in the Land of Israel to which they had come *"to build and be built by it."* Yosef Haim Brenner (1881-1921) and Shmuel Yosef Agnon (1888-1970), who propelled Hebrew prose into the 20th century, are considered by many to be the fathers of modern Hebrew literature, although they acted neither alone nor out of historical context.

Brenner, torn between hope and despair, struggled with his doubts concerning the difficulties of the Zionist enterprise in the Land of Israel and the low spiritual quality of certain sectors within the *yishuv* – the Jewish community in Palestine (Land of Israel) prior to the establishment of the state. He saw flaws everywhere and feared future developments with regard to the encounter between the Jewish and Arab populations of the area. In his endeavor to capture reality, he favored the rabbinical and medieval forms of spoken Hebrew, creating new idioms and employing dramatic syntax to give the effect of living speech. Central to Brenner's works is his identification with both the physical struggle of the pioneers

The biennial Jerusalem Book Fair, one of the world's leading book trade events, with the participation of some 1,000 publishers

Hebrew Book Week, which turns squares and parks into crowded book markets in cities, towns and villages throughout the country

for a toehold in an arid, harsh land, very different from the European countries where they were born, and the struggle, no less difficult, to shape the identity of the Jew in the Land of Israel.

Agnon chose to use more modern forms of the Hebrew language in his works. His familiarity with Jewish tradition, together with the influence of 19th and early 20th century European literature, gave rise to a body of fiction dealing with major contemporary spiritual concerns, the disintegration of traditional ways of life, the loss of faith and the subsequent loss of identity. An orthodox Jew and a writer of intuition and psychological insight, Agnon expressed an affinity for the shadowy and irrational sides of the human psyche and an identification with the inner uncertainties of the believing and non-believing Jew. Reality, as depicted by Agnon, exudes a tragic, at times grotesque ambience, with war and the Holocaust influencing much of his work, and the world of pious Jews revealed with all its passions and tensions. In 1966, Agnon was co-recipient of the Nobel

Prize for Literature (together with Nelly Sachs), the first Nobel Prize granted to an Israeli.

Native-born writers, who began publishing in the 1940s and 1950s, and are often referred to as 'the War of Independence Generation,' brought to their work a different mentality and cultural background from that of their predecessors, primarily because Hebrew was their mother tongue and their life experience was fully rooted in the Land of Israel. Authors such as S. Yizhar, Moshe Shamir, Hanoch Bartov, Chaim Gouri and Benjamin Tammuz vacillated dramatically between individualism and commitment to society and state, and presented a model of social realism, often in the heroic mode, featuring a blend of local and international influences.

In the early 1960s, new approaches in Hebrew prose writing were explored by a group of younger and very influential writers, including A.B. Yehoshua, Amos Oz, Yoram Kaniuk and Yaakov Shabtai, marking a break from ideological patterns and focusing on the world of the individual. During the next two decades, experimentation with narrative forms and various prose writing styles, including psychological realism, allegory and symbolism, as well as speculation and skepticism regarding Israel's political and social conventions, featured prominently in contemporary writing.

The 1980s and 1990s have witnessed a burst of intense literary activity in which the number of books published increased dramatically. Concurrently, several Israeli writers achieved international recognition, notably Oz, Yehoshua, Kaniuk, Aharon Appelfeld, David Shahar, David Grossman and Meir Shalev. A belief in literature as a means of enabling readers to understand themselves as individuals and as part of their environment characterizes the prose of this period, written by three generations of contemporary authors.

Renewed efforts to cope with the tragedy of the European Holocaust have brought about the formulation of fresh modes of expression to treat fundamental questions which can be discussed only within the perspective of time and place, integrating distance with involvement (Appelfeld, Grossman, Yehoshua Kenaz, Alexander and Yonat Sened, Nava Semel and others).

Previously unprobed themes have also been introduced, including the milieu of the Arab village (Anton Shammas, an Arab-Christian writer), the world of ultra-Orthodox Jews who deliberately segregate themselves from modern society (Yossl

The Institute for the Translation of Hebrew Literature was set up in 1962 to acquaint foreign readers and publishers with the best of contemporary Hebrew literature. Under its auspices, hundreds of works of fiction, poetry, drama and books for children have been published in some 40 languages – from German and Welsh to Hindi and Chinese. Institute projects range from putting together anthologies to organizing translators' conferences and participating in international book fairs. The Institute's computerized database and annual bibliographies of Hebrew literature in translation provide information to researchers world-wide. The Institute also publishes *Modern Hebrew Literature*, a biennial English-language journal.

Birstein), the way of life in Jerusalem's Hassidic courts (Haim Be'er) and attempts to deal with the existence of the unbeliever in a period when secular ideologies are collapsing and religious fundamentalism is gaining strength (Yitzhak Auerbach-Orpaz). Another important topic which some Israeli authors, themselves of Sephardic background, are addressing is the place in society of alienated new immigrants from Arab countries (Sami Michael, Albert Suissa, Dan Benaya-Seri). Others explore universal themes such as democracy and righteousness as seen in the context of a society which is subject to constant challenges in most areas of its national life (Yitzhak Ben Ner, Kaniuk, Grossman, Oz).

A number of major women authors have recently come to the fore, writing not only on general topics but also dealing with the world of women aware of their place in Jewish tradition and their role in the Zionist enterprise (Amalia Kahana-Carmon, Chana Bat Shachar, Shulamit Hareven, Shulamit Lapid, Ruth Almog, Savion Leibrecht, Batya Gur). Lapid and Gur have also entered the genre of detective fiction to critical

acclaim, both in Israel and in translation abroad.

Recently a younger generation of writers, who reject much of the centrality of the Israeli experience and reflect a more universalistic trend, often of an alienated, surreal and idiosyncratic nature, has emerged. Some of these writers enjoy almost cult followings, and their new books are assured a place at the top of the bestseller lists (Yehudit Katzir, Etgar Keret, Orly Castel-Blum, Gadi Taub, Irit Linor, Mira Magen).

In addition to the prolific body of Hebrew literature, a significant amount of writing, both prose and poetry, appears in other languages, including Arabic, English and French. Since the recent immigration of over 700,000 Jews from the former Soviet Union, Israel has become the largest center of literary creativity in the Russian language outside Russia itself.

During the last few years, Israeli publishers have entered the field of electronic publishing (multimedia, CD-ROM) in a massive way. Covering a wide range of topics, Israeli programs are being marketed worldwide.

POETRY

Written without interruption from biblical times to the present, Hebrew poetry embodies external influences and internal traditions. The poetry of the past, which incorporates religious and national themes, also contains motifs of personal experience which are predominant in the poetry of today. A break with traditional poetic expression developed during the Jewish Enlightenment in Europe (1781-1881), when full citizenship for Jews and secularization of Jewish life were advocated, and from the late 19th century when Zionism, the movement calling for the restoration of Jewish national life in the Land of Israel, began to gain momentum. The major poets to emerge from this period, who themselves immigrated to Palestine early in the 20th century, were Haim Nahman Bialik (1873-1934) and Saul Tchernichovsky (1875-1943).

Bialik's works, which reflect his commitment to the Jewish national renaissance and reject the viability of Jewish life in Eastern Europe, include both long epic poems recapitulating chapters in Jewish history as well as pure lyrical poetry dealing with love and nature. Bialik, often referred to as the 'national poet' or 'the poet of the Hebrew Renaissance,' forged a new poetic idiom, free of

---

צָנַח לוֹ זַלְזַל

צָנַח לוֹ זַלְזַל עַל־גָּדֵר וַיָּנָם —
כֹּה יָשֵׁן אָנֹכִי:
נָשַׁל הַפְּרִי — וּמַה־לִי וּלְגִזְעִי,
וּמַה־לִּי וּלְשׂוֹכִי?

נָשַׁל הַפְּרִי, הַפֶּרַח כְּבָר נִשְׁכָּח —
שָׂרְדוּ הֶעָלִים —
יִרְגְּזוּ יוֹם אֶחָד הַסַּעַר — וְנָפְלוּ
אַרְצָה חֲלָלִים.

אַחַר — וְנִמְשְׁכוּ לֵילוֹת הַזְּוָעָה,
לֹא מְנוּחָה וּשְׁנָת לִי,
בָּדָד אֶתְחַבֵּט בָּאֹפֶל וַאֲרַצֵּץ
רֹאשִׁי אֶל־הַתְּלִי.

וְשׁוּב יִפְרַח אָבִיב, וְאָנֹכִי לְבַדִּי
עַל־גִּזְעִי אֶתָּלֶה —
שַׁרְבִיט קֵרֵחַ, לֹא צִיץ לוֹ וָפֶרַח,
לֹא פְרִי וְלֹא־עָלֶה.

חַיִּים נַחְמָן בְּיַאלִיק

A Twig Alighted

A twig alighted on a fence and dozed;
So do I sleep.
The fruit fell — and what have I to do with
  my trunk,
What with my branch?

The fruit fell, the flower is already forgotten,
The leaves survive.
One day the storm will rage, they will drop
To the ground, dead.

Afterwards, the nights of dread go on,
No rest or sleep for me,
Alone I thrash about in the dark, smashing
My head against my wall.

And again spring blossoms,
And alone I hang from my trunk —
A bare shoot, without bud or flower,
Without fruit or leaf.

Haim Nahman Bialik
Translation: T. Carmi

עָמָל	Toil
הַלְבִּישִׁינִי, אִמָּא כְּשֵׁרָה, כְּתֹנֶת פַּסִּים לְתִפְאֶרֶת וְעִם שַׁחֲרִית הוֹבִילִינִי אֱלֵי עָמָל.	Dress me, good mother, in a glorious robe of many colors, And at dawn lead me to [my] toil.
עוֹטְפָה אַרְצִי אוֹר כַּטַּלִּית, בָּתִּים נִצְּבוּ כַטּוֹטָפוֹת, וְכִרְצוּעוֹת תְּפִלִּין גּוֹלְשִׁים כְּבִישִׁים, סָלְלוּ כַּפַּיִם.	My land is wrapped in light as in a prayer shawl, The houses stand forth like frontlets, And the roads paved by hand stream down like phylactery straps.
תְּפִלַּת שַׁחֲרִית פֹּה תִּתְפַּלֵּל קִרְיָה נָאָה אֱלֵי בּוֹרְאָהּ. וּבַבּוֹרְאִים — בְּנֵךְ אַבְרָהָם, פַּיְטָן-סוֹלֵל בְּיִשְׂרָאֵל.	Here the lovely city says the morning prayer to its Creator, And among the creators is your son Abraham, A road-building bard of Israel.
וּבְעֶרֶב בֵּין הַשְּׁמָשׁוֹת יָשׁוּב אַבָּא מִסִּבְלוֹתָיו וְכִתְפִלָּה יִלְחַשׁ נָחַת: — הַבֵּן יַקִּיר לִי אַבְרָהָם, עוֹר וְגִידִים וַעֲצָמוֹת — הַלְלוּיָהּ.	And in the evening twilight, father will return from his travails, And, like a prayer, will whisper joyfully: 'My dear son Abraham, skin, sinews and bones — 'Hallelujah.'
הַלְבִּישִׁינִי, אִמָּא כְּשֵׁרָה, כְּתֹנֶת פַּסִּים לְתִפְאֶרֶת וְעִם שַׁחֲרִית הוֹבִילִינִי אֱלֵי עָמָל.	Dress me, good mother, in a glorious robe of many colors, And at dawn lead me to [my] toil.
אַבְרָהָם שְׁלוֹנְסְקִי	*Abraham Shlonsky* *Translation: T. Carmi*

the overwhelming biblical influence of his predecessors, while maintaining classical structure and clarity of expression through rich, learned but contemporary phrasing. His poems are memorized by generations of Israeli schoolchildren.

Tchernichovsky, who wrote lyric poetry, dramatic epics, ballads and allegories, sought to rectify the world of the Jew by injecting a spirit of personal pride and dignity as well as a heightened awareness of nature and beauty. His sense of language, which embodied an affinity for rabbinical Hebrew, was different from Bialik's idiom which integrated the biblical influence with the emerging conversational mode. Both Bialik and Tchernichovsky represent the transition from ancient Jewish poetry to the modern genre.

Avraham Shlonsky, Natan Alterman, Lea Goldberg, and Uri Zvi Greenberg headed the next generation of poets, who wrote in the years which preceded the establishment of the state and during the early years of statehood.

Shlonsky utilized a flood of images along with linguistic inventions in his poetry as well as in his prolific translations of classical poetry, especially from Russian. Alterman's works, many of which are noted for their political commentary, accompanied every stage of the development of the Jewish community and are characterized by richness of language and a variety of poetic forms, tone and rhyme, imagery and metaphor. Goldberg expanded the spectrum of lyricism in poems which speak of the city, nature and the human being in search of love, contact and attention. Greenberg, who wrote a poetry of despair and rage using fierce imagery and stylistic power, dealt mainly with nationalistic themes and the impact of the Holocaust. This group of poets was first to introduce the rhythms of everyday speech into Hebrew poetry. They revived old idioms and coined new ones, giving the ancient language a new flexibility and richness.

The poetry of this period, which was greatly influenced by Russian futurism and symbolism as well as by German expressionism, tended towards the classical structure and melodicism of ordered rhyming. It reflected images and landscapes of the poets' country of birth and fresh visions of their new country in a heroic mode, as well as memories from 'there' and the desire to sink roots 'here,' expressing, as Lea Goldberg wrote, *"the pain of two homelands."* Many of the poems were set to music and became an integral part of the country's national lore.

The first major woman poet in Hebrew was Rahel Bluwstein

עִם שַׁחַר

נֵבֶל מַיִם בַּיָד ; עַל הַשֶׁכֶם
מַעְדֵּר, מַגְרֵפָה וָסַל —
לְשָׂדוֹת רְחוֹקִים, לֶעָמָל.

מִיָמִין — הָרִים כְּמִשְׁמֶרֶת,
מֶרְחֲבֵי שְׂדֵמוֹת לְפָנַי,
וְרָנִים בִּי עֶשְׂרִים אֲבִיבָי.

מְנָת חֶלְקִי עַד הַגִּיעַ קִצִּי ;
קָמָתֵךְ הַזּוֹהֶרֶת בַּשֶׁמֶשׁ
וַעֲפַר דְּרָכַיִךְ. אַרְצִי.

רָחֵל

Dawn

A jug of water in the hand, and on
My shoulder - basket, spade and rake.
To distant fields - to toil my path I make.

Upon my right, the great hills fling
Protecting arms; before me - the wide fields!
And in my heart, my twenty Aprils sing ...

Be this my lot, until I be undone:
Dust of thy road, my land, and thy
Grain waving golden in the sun!

Rahel
Translation: Abraham M. Klein

בְּשׁוּבִי

לֹא אֶהְיֶה מִתְקַבֵּל בְּשׁוּבִי
בְּקוֹלוֹת יְלָדִים, בִּנְבִיחַת כֶּלֶב נֶאֱמָן
וּבְעָשָׁן כְּחַלְחַל, כְּמוֹ בָּאַגָּדוֹת.
לֹא יִקְרֶה לִי "וַיִּשָּׂא עֵינָיו וַיַּרְא", כְּמוֹ
שֶׁקָּרָה בַּתְּנַ"ךְ "וְהִנֵּה".

עָבַרְתִּי אֶת גְּבוּל הַיַּתְמוּת
וּכְבָר מִזְּמַן לֹא קוֹרְאִים לִי
חַיָּל מְשֻׁחְרָר. אֵינֶנִּי מוּגָן.

אֲבָל הִמְצֵאתִי אֶת הַבְּכִי הַיָּבֵשׁ.
וּמִי שֶׁהִמְצִיא אֶת הַבְּכִי הַיָּבֵשׁ בָּעוֹלָם,
הִמְצִיא אֶת הַתְחָלַת הַקֵּץ בָּעוֹלָם
אֶת הַסֶּדֶק וְהַהֶרֶס וְהַקֵּץ.

יְהוּדָה עַמִּיחַי

On My Return

I will not be greeted on my return
by children's voices, or by the barking
of a loyal dog, or by blue smoke rising
as it happens in legends.
There won't happen for me any "and he
lifted his eyes" - as
in the Bible - "and behold."

I have crossed the border of being an
  orphan.
It's a long time since they called me
an ex-serviceman.
I'm not protected anymore.

But I have invented the dry weeping
And who has invented this
has invented the beginning of the world's
  end,
the crack and the tumbling down and the
  end.

Yehuda Amichai
Translation by the author

(1890-1931), who was known simply as "Rahel." Her works established the normative foundation of women's Hebrew poetry as well as the public's expectations of this poetry. Its lyrical, short, emotional, intellectually unpretentious and personal style has prevailed, as seen in most of the works of her contemporaries and of later poets such as Dalia Ravikovitch and Maya Bejerano.

In the mid-1950s, a new group of younger poets emerged, with Hebrew as their mother tongue, headed by Yehuda Amichai, Natan Zach, Dan Pagis, T. Carmi and David Avidan. This group, tending towards understatement, a general retreat from collective experiences, free observation of reality and a colloquial style, shifted the main poetic influences from Pushkin and Schiller to modern English and American poetry. The works of Amichai, who has been extensively translated, are marked by his use of daily speech, irony and metaphysical metaphors. These became the hallmarks of much of the poetry written by his younger contemporaries, who proclaimed the end of ideological poetry and broke completely with the Alterman-Shlonsky tradition of classical structures and ordered rhyming. Zach's works elicit innovative near-liturgical and musical qualities from everyday spoken Hebrew.

The field of Hebrew poetry today is a polyphony comprised of several generations, placing writers in their twenties together with poets of middle age. Representative of the latter group are Meir Wieselthier, whose prosaic, slangy and direct diction repudiates all romanticism and elevates the image of Tel Aviv as the symbol of reality; Yair Horowitz, whose restrained verses express the gentle sadness of one aware of his own mortality: and Yona Wallach, who presents herself in colloquial, sarcastic tones, using archetypal motifs, Freudian symbolism, sometimes brutal sensuality, rhythmic repetitions and long strings of associations. Other major contemporary poets include Asher Reich, Arieh Sivan, Ronny Somak and Moshe Dor.

בֻּבָּה מְמֻכֶּנֶת

בַּלַּיְלָה הַזֶּה הָיִיתִי בֻּבָּה מְמֻכֶּנֶת
וּפָנִיתִי יָמִינָה וּשְׂמֹאלָה, לְכָל הָעֲבָרִים,
וְנָפַלְתִּי אַפַּיִם אַרְצָה וְנִשְׁבַּרְתִּי לִשְׁבָרִים
וְנִסּוּ לְאַחוֹת אֶת שְׁבָרַי בְּיָד מְאֻמֶּנֶת.

וְאַחַר־כָּךְ שַׁבְתִּי לִהְיוֹת בֻּבָּה מְתֻקֶּנֶת
וְכָל מִנְהָגִי הָיָה שָׁקוּל וְצַיְתָנִי,
אוּלָם אָז כְּבָר הָיִיתִי בֻּבָּה מִסּוּג שֵׁנִי
כְּמוֹ זְמוֹרָה חֲבוּלָה שֶׁהִיא עוֹד אֲחוּזָה
בִּקְנוֹקֶנֶת.

וְאַחַר־כָּךְ הָלַכְתִּי לִרְקֹד בְּנֶשֶׁף הַמְּחוֹלוֹת
אַךְ הִנִּיחוּ אוֹתִי בְּחֶבְרַת חֲתוּלִים וּכְלָבִים
וְאִלּוּ כָּל צְעָדַי הָיוּ מְדוּדִים וּקְצוּבִים.

וְהָיָה לִי שֵׂעָר זָהָב וְהָיוּ לִי עֵינַיִם כְּחֻלּוֹת
וְהָיְתָה לִי שִׂמְלָה מִצֶּבַע פִּרְחֵי הַגַּן
וְהָיָה לִי כּוֹבַע שֶׁל קַשׁ עִם קִשּׁוּט דֻּבְדְּבָן.

דָּלְיָה רָבִיקוֹבִיץ׳

Mechanical Doll

On that night I was a mechanical doll turning right and left, in all directions, and I fell flat on my face and was broken to bits, and they tried to put my parts together with skillful hands.

And after that I again became a proper doll, and my bearing, at all times, was poised and submissive. But by then I was already a different sort of doll, like an injured twig, still held fast by a tendril.

And afterwards I went to dance at a ball, but they put me in the company of cats and dogs, yet all my steps were measured and fixed.

And I had golden hair and I had blue eyes and I had a dress the color of garden flowers and I had a straw hat with an ornamental cherry.

Dalia Ravikovitch
Translation: T. Carmi

18-23/3/95 פסטיבל משוררים בינלאומי ירושלים, משכנות שאננים
International Poets' Festival Jerusalem, Mishkenot Sha'ananim

The poetry of the most recent generation is dominated by individualism
and perplexity, and tends towards
short poems written in colloquial diction, non-rhymed free rhythm. Poetry
in Israel has a large and loyal reader-
ship and some volumes of poems, of
all periods, are sold in editions as
large as those published in much
more populous Western countries.

שִׁיר אֲדָמָה

Song of the Earth

מִמְּעוּף הַפֶּנְטְהָאוּז אֵין רוֹאִים
אֶת חֶמְדַּת הָאֲדָמָה שֶׁהֹרַגְנוּ עָלֶיהָ.

From the view of the penthouse you don't see
the delight of the earth over which we were killed.

זוֹ הָאֲדָמָה שֶׁאֲנִי מְבָרֵךְ עָלֶיהָ בְּקוֹמָה רָמָה
חַי עַל רְגָבֶיהָ וּמִתְאָרֵךְ בְּשִׁפְעַת צְלָלֶיהָ,
אֲדָמָה הוֹמִיָּה שֶׁאֲנִי כְּחוֹמָה חַיָּה מֵעָלֶיהָ
הוֹלֵךְ וְסוֹכֵךְ בַּחַמָּה עָלֶיהָ וְכוֹרֵךְ חַיֵּי
נְשִׁימָה נְשִׁימָה עָלֶיהָ. זוֹ הָאֲדָמָה שֶׁאֲנִי
שׁוֹפֵךְ דָּמִי עָלֶיהָ וּמְהַלֵּךְ בָּהּ אֶת יָמַי בִּדְמָמָה
וְנוֹסֵךְ עָלֶיהָ אֶת יִפְעַת זַרְעִי אַחֲרַי
אֲדָמָה שֶׁאֲנִי דּוֹרֵךְ עָלֶיהָ
וּמַשְׁקִיט גּוּמָה גּוּמָה כְּאֵב פְּצָעֶיהָ.
זוֹ הָאָרֶץ שֶׁאֲנִי שָׂרִיד וּפָלִיט
חַי כַּשְּׁמָמָה מֵעָלֶיהָ דּוֹעֵךְ וְהוֹלֵךְ
וְהַשָּׁמַיִם שָׁמַיִם לַה׳.

This is the earth over which I bless with lofty stature,
live on its clods and stretch out in the abundance
   of its shadows,
earth humming while I like a living wall
walk on it and cover it and bind my life
breath after beath over it. This is the earth
   over which I
spill my blood and walk all my days in quiet
and anoint with the splendour of my seed after me.
Earth that I tread on
and show painful wounds I silence pit after pit.
This is the land that I remnant and refugee
live on like a wasteland expiring and going out
and the heavens are the heavens of the Lord.

אשר רייך

Asher Reich
Translated by Linda Zisquit

CHILDREN'S LITERATURE

Children's literature, which includes original texts as well as translations of classics from many languages, integrates a wide variety of topics and prose styles, reflecting a world trend towards a more direct and sophisticated approach to language and intellectual content in writing for children.

During the first decade of the state, most Hebrew books for children focused on the prevailing social values of pioneering, struggle and achievement, emphasizing the individual's obligation to the building of the country. They were full of slogans and admiration of heroes, with the national vision occupying a central place. More often than not, authors tended to used the pronoun 'we' rather than 'I.'

Since the late 1960s, transmission of adult values in children's literature was gradually replaced with the world of the children themselves, dealing with topics such as death, divorce, single-parent families, handicaps, adolescence and the struggle for one's place in the family and society. At the same time, many imaginative children's books and stories were also written, providing young readers with pure fantasy, entertainment and escapism.

Motivating open inquiry and encouraging independent thinking have become basic elements in contemporary writing for children. While themes of social and national significance are still important, they are now treated with greater sincerity and openness. Some current books aim at negating stereotypes in the country's diversified society and deal with the immigration of Jews from many parts of the world, while others feature historical works and biographies which focus primarily on prominent figures who contributed to the development of the country over the last century,

beginning with the renewal of Jewish life in the Land of Israel.

Over the years a considerable body of children's literature for various age groups has been produced. It is distinguished by well-designed graphics and characterized by psychological sensitivity as well as by an expressive and picturesque use of language, enabling the young reader to identify with the substance of the writing in a dynamic way. Many Israeli books for children are now also being published in translation around the world, in a wide variety of languages.

FINE ARTS

From the beginning of the 20th century, fine arts in Israel have shown a creative orientation influenced by the encounter between East and West, as well as by the Land itself and its development, the character of the cities and stylistic trends emanating from art centers abroad. In painting, sculpture, photography and other art forms, the country's varied landscape is the protagonist: The hill terraces and ridges produce special dynamics of line and shape; the foothills of the Negev, the prevailing grayish-green vegetation and the clear luminous light result in distinctive color effects; and the sea and sand affect surfaces. On the whole, local landscapes, concerns and politics as well as the very nature of Israeli existentialism lie at the center of Israeli art and ensure its uniqueness.

Organized art activity in the country began in 1906, the year Professor Boris Schatz (1867-1932) arrived from Bulgaria and founded the Bezalel Academy of Arts and Crafts in Jerusalem, according to a plan approved at the 1905 Zionist Congress to encourage talented young Jews to study art in the Land of Israel. By 1910, the school had 32 different departments, a student body of 500 and a ready market for its works throughout the Jewish world.

In addition to painters and sculptors, the country's artistic life comprises a host of talented craftspeople (ceramicists, silver- and goldsmiths, weavers, calligraphers, glass blowers etc.), many of whom specialize in modern interpretations of traditional Jewish ceremonial objects.

Enthusiasm for art prevails among people from all walks of life, as Israelis encourage and support art activities by attending exhibits – from one-artist retrospectives to comprehensive group shows at the country's many museums and private galleries – by frequenting artists' quarters of Safad and Yafo or the artists' village of Ein Hod, and by purchasing the works of local artists.

PAINTING

At the outset, Bezalel's artistic orientation, which aimed at creating an 'original Jewish art' by fusing European techniques with Middle Eastern influences, resulted in paintings of biblical scenes depicting romanticized perceptions of the past linked to utopian visions of the future, with images drawn from the ancient Jewish Eastern communities as well as from the local Bedouin. Artists of this period include Shmuel Hirszenberg (1865-1908), Ephraim Lilien (1874-1925) and Abel Pann (1883-1963).

The first major art exhibition (1921), held at David's Citadel in Jerusalem's Old City, was dominated by painters from Bezalel. Soon afterwards, however, Bezalel's anachronistic, national-oriental narrative style was challenged both by young rebels within the Bezalel establishment and

Abel Pann: *Study for Abraham*

Nahum Gutman: *Arab Woman*

newly-arrived artists, who began searching for an idiom appropriate to what they termed 'Hebrew' as opposed to 'Jewish' art. In an attempt to define their new cultural identity and express their view of the country as a source of national renewal, they depicted the daily reality of the Near Eastern environment, with emphasis on the bright light and glowing colors of the landscape, and stressed exotic subject matter such as the simple Arab lifestyle through a predominantly primitive technique, as seen in the works of painters including Israel Paldi, Tziona Tagger, Pinhas Litvinovsky, Nahum Gutman and Reuven Rubin.

By the middle of the decade, most of the leading artists were established in the new, dynamic city of Tel Aviv (est. 1909), which has remained the center of the country's artistic activity.

The art of the 1930s was strongly influenced by early 20th century Western innovations, the most powerful of which was the expressionism emanating from the ateliers of Paris. Works of painters such as Moshe Castel, Menachem Shemi and Arie Aroch tended to portray an emotionally charged, often mystical reality through their use of distortion and, although themes still dealt with local landscapes and images, the narrative components of ten years earlier gradually disappeared and the oriental-Moslem world vanished entirely. German expressionism was introduced in the middle of the decade with the arrival of immigrant artists fleeing the terror of rising Nazism. Joining German-born artists Anna Ticho and Leopold Krakauer who had come to Jerusalem some 20 years earlier, this group, which included Hermann Struck, Mordechai Ardon and Jakob Steinhardt, devoted itself largely to subjective interpretations of the landscape of Jerusalem and the surrounding hills. These artists made a significant contribution to the development of local art, notably through the leadership given to the Bezalel

Arieh Aroch: *The High Commissioner*

Academy of Art by its directors, Ardon and Steinhardt, under whose guidance a new generation of artists grew to maturity.

The break with Paris during World War II and the trauma of the Holocaust caused several artists, including Moshe Castel, Yitzhak Danziger and Aharon Kahana, to adopt the emerging 'Canaanite' ideology which sought to identify with the original inhabitants of the land and create a 'new Hebrew people' by reviving ancient myths and pagan motifs. The 1948 War of Independence led other artists, including Naftali Bezem and Avraham Ofek, to adopt a militant style with a clear social message. But the most significant group formed in this period was 'New Horizons,' which aimed to free Israeli painting from its local character and literary associations and bring it into the sphere of contemporary European art. Two major trends developed: Yosef Zaritzky, the group's dominant figure, tended towards an atmospheric lyricism, characterized by the presence of identifiable fragments of local landscape and cool color tones. His style was adopted by others, notably Avigdor Stematsky and Yehezkel Streichman. The second trend, a stylized abstractionism ranging from geometricism to a formalism frequently based on symbols, was

Mordechai Ardon: Towards Jerusalem

strongly evident in the works of the Romanian-born artist Marcel Janco, who studied in Paris and was one of the founders of Dadaism. The New Horizons group not only legitimized abstract art in Israel but was also its dominant force up to the early 1960s.

Artists of the 1960s provided the connecting link between the activities of the New Horizons group and the search for individuality in the next decade. Streichman and Stematsky, both teachers at the Avni Institute in Tel Aviv, strongly influenced a second generation of artists, including Raffi Lavi, Aviva Uri, Uri Lifschitz and Lea Nikel who, in their search for a personal imagery, challenged the refined brushwork of lyrical abstractionism with pluralistic works, encompassing various expressive and figurative abstract styles derived from sources abroad. At Bezalel, Ardon's influence, especially with regard to themes and techniques, evidenced itself in the works of Avigdor Arikha, who developed a world of forms filled with intense spiritual meaning, and in the return to figurative themes evocative of the Holocaust and traditional Jewish subjects, as seen in the surrealistic paintings of Yossl Bergner and Samuel Bak.

Jacob Agam is a pioneer in optic and kinetic art, and his work is exhibited in many countries.

While the minimalism characteristic of art in the 1970s almost always included amorphic, transparent forms reminiscent of local abstract painting, the exposition of ideas rather than aesthetics dominated the works of artists such as Larry Abramson and Moshe Gershuni. The artists of the 1980s and 1990s, working in an atmosphere of individual experimentation, appear to be searching for content and a sense of Israel's spirit by integrating a wide range of materials and techniques, as well as images based on local and universal elements as diverse as the letters of the Hebrew alphabet and the human emotions of stress and fear. Current trends, as in the work of Pinhas Cohen-Gan, Deganit Beresht, Gabi Klasmer, Tsibi Geva, Tzvi Goldstein, David Reeb and others, continue to strive towards broadening the definition of Israeli art beyond its traditional concepts and materials, both as the unique expression of an indigenous culture and as a dynamic component of contemporary Western art.

Larry Abramson: *Column III*

234

Photography in Israel today, characterized by intimacy, restraint and a preoccupation with the self, is both a reaction to and an outgrowth of the romantic, informational style which dominated its early stages of development. In the mid-19th century, local photography was based largely on providing photographic services, concentrating on the depiction of holy places (mainly Christian) to sell as souvenirs to pilgrims and tourists.

From 1880 onwards, photographers began to document the development of the Jewish community in Palestine (Land of Israel), portraying the pioneers working the soil and building cities and towns, through a heroic lens, oriented to a modern, secular ideology and the requirements of clients who used their pictures to further particular causes such as the Jewish National Fund.

The country's development in its early years was faithfully recorded by a number of talented photojournalists, some still active today, including Tim Gidal, David Rubinger, Werner Braun, Boris Carmi, Zev Radovan, David Harris and Micha Bar Am. Crossing the invisible boundary between 'photography as documentation' and 'art photography' are, among others, Aliza Auerbach who concentrates on portraiture; Neil Folberg, Doron Horwitz and Shai Ginott who focus on nature, David Darom, an expert underwater photographer; and Dubi Tal and Mony Haramati, a team specializing in aerial photography.

In recent years, as photography as a pure artistic medium has become a legitimate art form, a number of creative photographers have emerged, with the active support of galleries, museums, curators and collectors. Today's art photography is highly personal, probing questions of life and death, art and illusion, in styles ranging from the formalistic and minimalistic to the pictorial and intellectual-conceptual. Several important venues for displaying photographic work have come into being, foremost among them being the photography biennale at Mishkan Le'Omanut at Kibbutz Ein Harod and the new Museum of Photography at Tel Hai in the northern Galilee.

Dani Karavan: *The White City*

SCULPTURE

The art of sculpture flourished in the country due to the efforts of a few sculptors over a long period of time. While Avraham Melnikoff, known for his massive stone lion at Tel Hai, and Ze'ev Ben-Zvi introduced cubism, the more academic school of sculpture, represented by Moshe Ziffer, Aharon Priver and Batya Lishansky, dominated the field prior to the establishment of the state.

At the end of the 1940s, the 'Canaanite' ideology influenced a number of artists, notably Yitzhak Danziger whose figure of the pagan hero-hunter Nimrod, carved from red Nubian sandstone, is an attempt to create a synthesis between Middle Eastern sculpture and the modern concept of the human body, while the forms comprising his sculpture of sheep resemble those of desert rocks, water canals and Bedouin tents. Sculpture in the 1950s employed new materials and monumental scale as it became increasingly abstract, stimulated in part by the recent introduction of iron and corten steel as a sculptural medium.

The desire to provide a tangible memorial to those who fell in Israel's wars gave sculpture a new impetus from the 1960s on, and a great many monuments, primarily nonfigurative, were introduced into the Israeli landscape. This genre is represented by Yehiel Shemi's welded steel naval memorial at Achziv, which deals both with the harshness of nature and the human capacity for violence and destruction, and Dani Karavan's "Monument to the Negev Brigade" outside Be'er Sheva, evoking the special character of desert combat.

Under the influence of the French school in general and expressionism in particular, and utilizing a wide range of materials, contemporary conceptual artists are creating installations and environmental sculptures to depict their individual reactions to social and political realities. Incorporating a powerful play of shapes and symbols, the works of Yigal Tumarkin express his protest against war through geometric and figurative abstract forms, while the trend towards geometric minimalism is especially pronounced in Menashe Kadishman's persistent use of the images of sheep, which call up both a local pastoral image and a personal myth symbolizing the helpless victim.

Several Israeli sculptors have gained international recognition, including Tumarkin, Karavan, Kosso Eloul and Israel Hadany, whose works can be seen in public and private settings abroad.

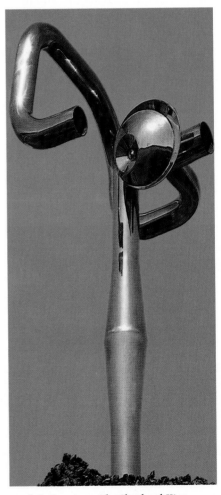

Yitzhak Danziger: *The Shepherd King*

MUSEUMS

Some 120 museums around the country record nearly ten million visits a year. Large or small, in city, town or kibbutz, they are treasure houses of archaeology, ethnography and local history; of art, both ancient and modern; and of crafts, from primitive to sophisticated.

Museums established in recent years include the galleries and open-air sculpture exhibition at the Tefen Industrial Park in Upper Galilee, the Museum of Israeli Art in Ramat Gan, the Museum of Bedouin Culture near Be'er Sheva, the Tower of David Museum of the History of Jerusalem and the Bible Lands Museum in Jerusalem, the Hecht Museum in Haifa, the museum of the Allon Center at Kibbutz Ginossar and the Museum of Photography at Tel Hai.

At the Youth Wing

The Israel Museum in Jerusalem, founded (1965) as the country's national museum, comprises several main sections: the collection of the Bezalel Museum of Fine Arts, Judaica and Ethnography, exhibits of items typical of various Diaspora Jewish communities, art galleries, period rooms and a comprehensive selection of art objects from Africa, North and South America, Oceania and the Far East; an archaeological wing containing artifacts from prehistoric times to the 15th century CE; a sculpture garden with over 60 works; the Shrine of the Book which houses rare biblical manuscripts, including the Dead Sea Scrolls; a youth wing comprising galleries, classrooms and workshops, with an extensive educational program; the Rockefeller Museum in East Jerusalem, housing a collection of regional archaeology; the Paley Art Center in East Jerusalem which runs programs for Arab children; and the Ticho House, an art gallery and popular cafe in a century-old mansion in the center of Jerusalem. A wide range of temporary exhibitions are presented regularly, as well as activities ranging from lectures, workshops and films to chamber concerts and art classes.

The Tel Aviv Museum of Art (est. 1932), which opened its present building in 1971, consists of four central galleries housing a comprehensive collection of classical and contemporary art, especially Israeli art; a youth wing; an auditorium where recitals, chamber concerts and art films are presented regularly; and numerous halls which feature temporary exhibits. The Helena Rubinstein Pavilion of Modern Art is also under its aegis.

Mishkan la-Omanut ("Home of Art," est. 1934), at Kibbutz Ein Harod, the first rural museum in the country and the first art museum of the kibbutz movement, houses an extensive collection of Jewish painting, sculpture and folk art from all over the world, features special temporary exhibitions and carries out various educational projects and art research.

The Haifa Museum houses three museums in a single building: the Museum of Ancient Art (est. 1949), which specializes in archaeological finds discovered in Israel and the Mediterranean basin; the Museum of Modern Art (est. 1951), with exhibits of art from all over the world (mid-18th century to the present); and the Museum of Music and Ethnography, featuring exhibits of musical instruments through the ages and costumes from various Diaspora Jewish communities, as well as from the Arab and Druze communities near Haifa. Also under the Museum's aegis are the Museum of Prehistory, the National Maritime Museum and the recently renovated Tikotin Museum of Japanese Art.

The Negev Museum (est. 1953) in Be'er Sheva, housed in a number of structures built in Turkish times, consists of a modern art wing and an archaeology section, featuring items representative of periods of settlement in the region. An exhibit of archaeological finds from the biblical city of Be'er Sheva (c.900 BCE) is displayed at Tel Sheva.

The Eretz Israel Museum (est. 1953) in Ramat Aviv, a comprehensive storehouse of archaeological, anthropological and historical findings in the region, comprises pavilions for glassware, ceramics, coins, folklore and copper, among others, as well as a planetarium. The 'Man and His Work' section features live demonstrations of ancient methods of weaving, jewelry and pottery making, grain grinding and bread baking. Tel Quasile, an excavation in which 12 distinct layers of civilization have been uncovered, is on the site. Also under the Museum's aegis are the Museum of the History of Tel Aviv-Jaffa and Independence Hall, where the State of Israel was proclaimed in 1948, both of which are in central Tel Aviv.

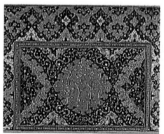

The L.A. Mayer Institute for Islamic Art (est. 1974) in Jerusalem houses extensive permanent exhibitions of pottery, textiles, jewelry, ceremonial objects and the like, covering a thousand years of Islamic art, from Spain to India, and features temporary exhibits on special themes.

Beit Hatefutsot (The Diaspora Museum, est. 1978), located on the Tel Aviv University campus, uses modern techniques and audio-visual displays to trace the history of Diaspora Jewish communities through the ages and throughout the world. In this non-artifact museum, exhibitions are arranged thematically, and each floor has a study area. Temporary exhibits on Jewish subjects, a chronosphere presenting an audio-visual overview of Jewish history and a full range of educational and cultural programs and traveling exhibitions are also regularly featured.

The Tower of David Museum of the History of Jerusalem (est. 1988) is located in the Citadel compound, an important historical and archaeological site containing finds from the First Temple Period (960-586 BCE), parts of a tower and the city wall from Hasmonean times (first century BCE), and the base of a huge tower built by Herod (37-4 BCE). The non-artifact museum covers 4,000 years of Jerusalem's history, from its beginnings as a Canaanite city to modern times. Exhibits are divided according to periods, with a 'time line' in each room depicting main events, as well as displays effected by means of maps, videotapes, holograms, drawings and models. Temporary exhibitions on related subjects are featured from time to time.

The Yad Vashem Museum in Jerusalem is dedicated to perpetuating the memory of the six million Jews who perished in the Holocaust. It includes an art gallery, the Hall of Names, the Avenue of Righteous Gentiles, an archive, the central remembrance hall with names of the extermination camps on the floor, the Children's Memorial Pavilion and the Valley of the Destroyed Communities.

The Israel Philharmonic Orchestra

MUSIC

Israel is one of the world's most active centers of musical activity, with a diversified classical music life based on the talents of composers and thousands of professional musicians as well as a unique and dynamic folk music genre generated by its immigrant society.

CLASSICAL MUSIC

Music began to occupy an important place in the cultural life of the Jewish community in Palestine (Land of Israel) after World War I, with various attempts made by enthusiastic amateurs and a tiny cadre of trained musicians at forming a symphony orchestra, a choral society and even an opera company. Music on a professional level, however, became a major activity only in the 1930s when hundreds of music teachers and students, composers, instrumentalists and singers, as well as thousands of music lovers, streamed into the country, driven by the threat of Nazism in Europe.

The Palestine Philharmonic Orchestra (today the Israel Philharmonic Orchestra), founded at the initiative of Polish-born violinist Bronislaw Huberman, gave its first concert in Tel Aviv under the baton of Arturo Toscanini in 1936. It immediately became one of the pivots of the country's musical life and over the years acquired a reputation as one of the pre-eminent orchestras in the world. Soon after, a radio orchestra was established (today the Jerusalem Symphony Orchestra) whose broadcast concerts attracted tens of thousands of listeners. Additional musical organizations were founded at later dates, including the Israel Chamber Orchestra, the Be'er Sheva Sinfonietta and orchestras based in Haifa, Netanya, Holon, Ramat Gan and Rishon Lezion.

In the late 1980s, the New Israel Opera began mounting productions on a high professional level, reviving public enthusiasm for operatic works which had declined following the disbanding of the first permanent opera company some years earlier.

During the early 1990s, Israel's musical life underwent a transformation with the massive influx of over 700,000 Jews from the former Soviet Union. This immigration brought with it many professional musicians, including instrumentalists, singers and music teachers, whose impact is felt with the formation of new symphony and chamber orchestras, as well as smaller ensembles, and a dynamic injection of talent and musical vitality into educational frameworks in schools, conservatories and community centers throughout the country.

The chamber music tradition, which also began in the 1930s, includes a number of internationally acclaimed ensembles and choral groups, which have expanded in range and variety since the immigration of the 1990s. Leading groups include the Israel Chamber Orchestra,

whose members are drawn from kibbutzim throughout the country, the Rehovot Camerata, the chamber orchestra of the IDF Education Corps and the Kashtaniot Camerata of Ramat Hasharon. Many cities and towns sponsor their own choirs, and several festivals are devoted to choral music including Jerusalem's *Liturgica*, vocal music in the churches of Abu Ghosh and the Zimriya festival.

Musical performances, from recitals to full symphony concerts presenting a wide range of classical works, are held in historic settings like the restored Roman amphitheaters at Caesarea and Beit She'an, and in two major concert halls, the Mann Auditorium in Tel Aviv and Jerusalem's International Convention Center. Smaller venues include the Jerusalem Theater complex, Tel Aviv's new Performing Arts Center, the Tel Aviv

and Israel Museums as well as cultural centers in towns and kibbutzim throughout the country. Israeli concertgoers are enthusiastic and demonstrative, attributes much appreciated by the renowned guest musicians and world-famous Israeli soloists such as Pinhas Zuckerman, Shlomo Mintz, Daniel Barenboim and Itzhak Pearlman, who are part of the country's music scene every year.

World-class music events which take place in Israel include the International Harp Contest and the Artur Rubinstein Piano Competition. Local festivals such as the Music Festival at Kibbutz Ein Gev and the Chamber Music Festival at Kibbutz Kfar Blum draw appreciative audiences, while the Israel Festival, which features music, theater and dance performed by groups from all over the world, turns Jerusalem into a cultural magnet for three weeks each spring.

The creation of specifically Israeli music has been evolving since professional composing began in the country in the mid-1940s. While Russian and French traditions, German romantic and post-romantic forces, and the lively evocations of later European composers all left their mark on local compositions, a new expression of modern Israel in the so-called 'Mediterranean' style, integrating traditional Eastern melodies and the cantillation of ancient prayer, has gradually crystallized.

The first generation of Israeli composers, all European-born, made great efforts to write in a new musical idiom after immigrating to the country. Paul Ben-Haim utilized expanded tonalities to create a post-expressionistic style, welding old and new, East and West; Oedon Partos saw in the assimilation of authentic folklore an important compositional method; Alexander Uriah Boscovitch used popular forms of expression as a compositional building block; Yosef Tal founded electronic composition in Israel; and Mordechai Seter concentrated on integrating Yemenite melodies and rhythms into his works.

The second generation, most of them direct and indirect students of the first, have worked towards a musical expression which integrates the Hebrew language, with its consonants and intonation, its relevance to Jewish liturgy and tradition, and its incorporation into the Eastern world. The third and most recent group of composers manifest a desire to participate in international composition with no national profile, to grapple with the Holocaust through music and to break down barriers within music, merging Eastern and Western traditions and incorporating some innovations from popular music genres.

Talented young Israelis begin their training by attending one of some 200 conservatories or by studying with one of hundreds of private teachers; many gain experience by joining one of the country's youth orchestras. Further study is provided at the degree-granting academies for music and dance in Jerusalem and Tel Aviv. Master classes for singers, instrumentalists and chamber groups are frequently conducted by visiting international artists at the academies, as well as at the Jerusalem Music Center.

Music education and research at institutions of higher learning were inaugurated at the beginning of the 1960s with the establishment of the Artur Rubinstein Chair of Musicology at the Hebrew University of Jerusalem. Since then, musicology departments have been added also at Tel Aviv University and Bar llan University. Two major areas of specialization are offered: Jewish music and the music of Israel's various ethnic groups, with particular emphasis on the music of the Eastern/Sephardic communities.

שירים עד כאן, הבכי והצחוק קולות האנשים, כוכבי הזמן. השמש והים הלחם, העולם המר והמתוק וכל מה שהיה נשאיר לחיות בתוך השיר.	Songs so far Tears and laughter Voices of men, stars of time. The sun and the sea Bread, the world, The bitter, the sweet And everything that has been we shall leave To live within the song.
נתן יונתן	*Lyrics : Natan Yonatan*

SONGS

"The songs and I are friends for life" is not just a line in a lyric, but expresses the proprietary attitude of Israelis towards their songs. The early pioneers brought their songs with them, translating the original lyrics into Hebrew or setting new Hebrew words to treasured tunes. Since then, thousands of songs have been written, with melodies incorporating elements of the musical styles brought by consecutive waves of immigrants, ranging from Arab and Yemenite traditions to modern rock and pop, sometimes set to biblical or traditional texts or to the modern verses of Israeli poets and lyricists.

While it is difficult to define a typical Hebrew song, Israelis differentiate between songs written in Hebrew, on various themes and in a variety of styles, and the *Shir Ivri* ('Hebrew Song'), whose words transmit the voices, values and moods of the country and whose melodies are dominated by Slavic influences. Accompanying the major historical events in the national life of the Jewish people over the past century, these songs have recorded the nation's dreams, pains and hopes. While expressing universal sentiments like all folk songs, they also articulate strongly Israeli feelings such as love of the country and its landscape. These are the songs everyone knows, the songs which have become an integral part of the nation's cultural legacy.

Israelis love to sing their songs, from those of the pre-state period to ones just written. Community singing takes place in public halls and private homes, in kibbutz dining rooms and in community centers, during hikes and around bonfires, often under the guidance of a professional song leader, accompanied by

piano, accordion or guitar. Participation in such group singing generates a sense of togetherness, evoked by patriotic sentiments as well as by nostalgia for the early pioneering days and the struggle for independence, for wars won, friends lost and recurring moments of hope and love.

שירים לא עוזבים,
הם עוזרים לעבור,
אוהבים וזוכרים.
הם לא שוכחים
שצריך לחזור
בימים הקרים.
הם לא משתנים.
הם תמיד מתכונים
לכל מה שהם אומרים,
ולכן לעולם
נשאר השירים ואני חברים.

אהוד מנור

Songs do not leave,
They help you get by,
They love and remember.
They do not forget
that you've got to come back
on cold days.
They do not change.
They always mean
everything they say
and that is why we,
the songs and I,
are friends for life.

Lyrics: Ehud Manor

DANCE

In the communal and religious life of the Jewish people, dance has been regarded as an expression of joy since biblical times and is today an integral part of religious, national, community and family celebrations. Contemporary dance has developed in two directions: expansion of the folk dance genre which accompanied the early settlers in the rebuilding of their ancient homeland; and the establishment of art dance, leading to stage productions created by professional choreographers and performed by trained dancers.

ART DANCE

Dance as an art form was introduced in the country in the 1920s by newly-arrived teachers and devotees of dance from the cultural centers of Europe. After the establishment of the state, it was developed to a high professional level by a number of ensembles, each founded on the basis of a different orientation and style. Today six major professional dance companies, most of them based in Tel Aviv, perform a varied repertoire throughout the country and abroad.

The Inbal Dance Theater, Israel's oldest professional company, was established by its artistic director and chief choreographer Sara Levi-Tannai, and is now run by former star dancer Margalit Oved. Its repertoire, which often deals with biblical subjects, is largely based on movement material suggested by the dance, music and poetry traditions of Yemenite and other Eastern Jewish communities. Over the years, Inbal has performed widely abroad.

The Batsheva Dance Company, founded (1964) by Baroness Batsheva de Rothschild and Martha Graham, enjoys worldwide acclaim. The company has a unique repertoire, including daring dances choreographed by its artistic director, Ohad Naharin, and encourages artistic collaborations expanding the boundaries of dance. The Batsheva Ensemble, the training gound for Batsheva's apprentice dancers, is gaining a professional reputation of its own.

The Bat-Dor Dance Company, also set up by Baroness Batsheva de Rothschild with Jeanette Ordman as its artistic director, comprises about 20 dancers and features the works of some of the world's best-known choreographers, including Israeli-born Domy Reiter-Soffer. Dance schools in Tel Aviv and Be'er Sheva are attached to the company.

The Kibbutz Contemporary Dance Company based in Kibbutz Ga'aton in the northern Galilee, comprises dancers from different kibbutzim. Under the direction of its founder, Yehudit Arnon, this widely-acclaimed troupe performs a repertoire which includes the works of international and local choreographers, including kibbutz member Rami Be'er.

Kol-Dmama (Sound-Silence), a unique company comprised of deaf and hearing dancers, was founded (1978) by Moshe Efrati using a system for transmitting vibrations from dancer to dancer. With an original repertoire created by Efrati, the company has achieved an international following as well as making a significant contribution to the rehabilitation of the deaf.

The Israel Ballet grew out of a studio for classical dance set up by its artistic directors, Berta Yampolsky and Hillel Markman. The only professional classical ballet company in the country, it performs classical, neo-classical and contemporary works created by Yampolsky as well as ballets by Balanchine and other international choreographers.

The country's modern dance scene is further enhanced by a number of smaller groups mostly dependent on the potential of one artist such as the dance theater of Rina Schenfeld, the Yaron Margolin Dance Company, the dance duo Liat Dror and Nir Ben-Gal, the Tmu-Na Dance Theater Group, the Vertigo Dance Company and Tnuatron.

Since its opening in 1989, the Suzanne Dellal Center for Dance and Theater in the newly renovated Neve Tzedek quarter of Tel Aviv has become the focal point of dance activities in the country. Also in Tel Aviv, the Dance Library of Israel and the Israel Dance Archive, in addition to serving as centers for study and research, publish books on dance and the *Israel Dance Annual*. Training is offered by the dance departments of the Rubin Academies of Music and Dance in Jerusalem and Tel Aviv, the Bat-Dor Studios, the Talma Yellin school in Tel Aviv and a number of other dance schools and workshops throughout the country.

Israel's contributions to the field of movement education include the methods of Moshe Feldenkrais, which are taught all over the world, and the Eshkol-Wachman movement notation system, one of the three best-known systems of recording dance and movement in written form.

FOLK DANCE

Israeli folk dance emerged as an amalgam of Jewish and non-Jewish folk dance forms from many parts of the world. While in other countries folk dance is fostered to preserve old rural traditions, in Israel it is a constantly developing art form which has evolved since the 1940s, based on historic and modern sources as well as on biblical associations and contemporary dance styles.

The early pioneers, who exchanged urban life in Eastern Europe for rural life in a collective setting, brought with them native dances which were adapted to their new milieu. Among them, a Romanian dance, the *hora*, typified the new life being built in the Land of Israel: its closed circle form gave equal status to all participants, simple movements enabled everyone to take part and the linked arms symbolized the new ideology. Today it remains the representative Israeli dance, performed on occasions from street dancing on Independence Day to social gatherings.

The turning point in local folk dance development occurred at the first folk dance festival held at Kibbutz Dalia in 1944. Widespread enthusiasm for dance followed, bringing with it the creation of a multifaceted folk dance genre characterized by a combination of styles and sources.

Incorporated in it are Diaspora Jewish motifs and local traditions, including the Arab *debka*, a foot-stamping dance of men linked in a row, as well as dance elements ranging from North American jazz and Latin American rhythms to the cadences typical of Mediterranean countries.

The country's folk dances, most of which are set to popular Israeli songs, comprise a great variety of steps and forms, juxtaposed with exuberant movement, expressing the vitality and vivaciousness of a young country with an old tradition. Folk dance manifests itself both through individual participation and stage performances. Public enthusiasm for folk dancing has led to the emergence of the professional dance leader and to thousands of people participating regularly in dance activities as a recreational outlet. Many localities offer weekly folk dancing, with some of them sponsoring performing ensembles as well.

Alongside Israeli folk dance, and influencing it, are the traditional dances of the different ethnic groups, which reflect both the 'ingathering of the exiles' and the pluralistic nature of Israel's society. They are preserved by a number of troupes specializing in the dances of Yemen, Kurdistan, North Africa, India, Georgia, Bukhara and Ethiopia, and by ensembles which perform Arab, Druze and Circassian dances.

Folk dance troupes appear at most local and national celebrations, and perform at local and international festivals. Since 1988, a three-day international folk dance festival has been held annually at Karmiel, a town in central Galilee, with the participation of troupes from Israel and around the world.

THEATER

Hebrew theater, unlike literature, did not exist in ancient Hebrew culture, nor did it grow out of the Yiddish theater so popular in Eastern European Jewish communities up to World War II. It began with the founding in 1917 of a Hebrew theater, *Habimah* (The Stage) in Moscow, under the guidance of Russian director Constantin Stanislavsky and with the acting talent of Hanna Rovina (1892-1980), who later became recognized as the 'First Lady of Hebrew Theater.' In 1931, the company set up its permanent home in Tel Aviv.

Theater in Israel is composed of many different elements – contemporary and classical, indigenous and imported, experimental and traditional – with playwrights, actors, directors and producers of many backgrounds merging the foreign with the local and thereby gradually creating a distinctive Israeli theater. The theater scene is very active, with six professional repertory theaters and dozens of regional and amateur companies performing throughout the country to large and devoted audiences. In recent years, a number of Israeli companies have toured Eastern and Western Europe, participated in international festivals, including the Edinburgh Festival, and appeared in major theater events in Europe, the United States and elsewhere. A number of semi-professional and amateur groups perform in English and Russian.

Leading playwrights, several of whom have received international recognition, include Hanoch Levine, Yehoshua Sobel, Hillel Mittelpunt and Ephraim Kishon. The major professional companies are located in the country's four largest cities.

Habimah, the national theater, housed in a three-hall complex (total of 1,520 seats) in Tel Aviv, has an average attendance rate of about 90 percent, due in part to its over 30,000 annual subscribers. Its repertoire includes traditional plays on Jewish themes, works of contemporary Hebrew playwrights and translations of international classics, dramas and comedies, with internationally acclaimed directors sometimes brought in to stage local productions.

The Cameri Theater, the Tel Aviv municipal theater since 1970, was the first company to stage realistic portrayals of Israeli life and has continued to contribute to the development of Hebrew theater with a lively repertoire, including a major series of original Israeli dramas and adaptations of major theatrical hits.

The Haifa Municipal Theater, the first theater in the country to be publicly sponsored, is an adventurous and popular company best known for its performances of original Israeli works dealing with controversial and provocative themes.

The Be'er Sheva Municipal Theater tours throughout the country bringing theatrical productions to enthusiastic audiences. It is generally considered the most popular repertory theater for local drama school graduates to begin their professional careers.

The Khan Theater, Jerusalem's only repertory theater, offers a mixture of contemporary and classical works in a unique hall situated in a restored, centuries-old Turkish inn.

The Gesher Theater, founded in 1991 to provide an artistic outlet for new immigrants from the former Soviet Union, first offered high-level productions in Russian. Following its success and critical acclaim, it has now entered the mainstream of Israeli theater with Hebrew plays. It still employs mainly Russian-speaking performers and is a major factor in their integration into Israel's theatrical life.

The Children's and Youth Theater stages plays for three different age groups at schools and cultural centers throughout the country, conducts drama and theater classes and provides instructors for special school workshops.

A number of other theaters, including the Hasimta, Beit Liessin, Itim and kibbutz theaters, are experimental in nature and avant-garde in approach, with repertoires tending to focus on social satire and interpretation of current issues.

Many new playwrights and acting groups get a professional start by presenting works at the Festival of Alternative Theater, which takes place annually in Akko, in a setting enhanced by the halls and battlements of the Crusader city. An International Festival of Puppet Theater takes place each spring in Jerusalem.

Training in acting, directing and allied stage professions is available at Tel Aviv University, the Hebrew University of Jerusalem, the Beit-Zvi School for Arts, Stage and Cinema (Ramat Gan), the Nissan Nativ Acting Studio (Tel Aviv) and the Kibbutz Seminar's School of Drama.

CINEMA

Film-making in Israel has undergone major developments since its inception in the 1950s. While the first features produced and directed by Israelis such as "Hill 24 Does Not Answer," and "They Were Ten," tended, like literature, to be cast in the heroic mold of that period, some recent films are deeply rooted in the Israeli experience, such as Holocaust survivors and their children (Gila Almagor's "The Summer of Aviya" and its sequel, "Under the Domin Tree") and the travails of new immigrants ("Sh'hur," directed by Hannah Azoulai and Shmuel Hasfari, "Coffee with Lemon," directed by Leonid Gorivets). Others reflect a more

predominant trend towards present Israeli reality, whether dealing with the Israel-Arab confrontation (Uri Barbash's "Beyond the Walls") or set in the context of universalist, somewhat alienated and hedonistic society ("A Siren's Song," "Life According to Agfa," "Tel Aviv Stories").

Cinema exports are growing annually, as more Israeli-made films become successful abroad and more dollar-earning foreign and co-productions are filmed on location in the country. The Israel Film Center, a division of the Ministry of Trade and Industry, promotes filmmaking in Israel by both local and foreign producers and provides services, from arranging professional contacts to offering financial incentives.

The **Spielberg Film Archive** at the Hebrew University of Jerusalem is the world's largest repository of film material on Jewish themes as well as on Jewish and Israeli life. Run by the university together with the Central Zionist Archives, its main activity is collecting, preserving and cataloging Jewish films, and making the material available to researchers, film and television writers and producers throughout the world.

The **Jerusalem Cinemathéque** consists of an archive of thousands of films, a research library, viewing halls and exhibition space. It presents regular screenings, often in thematic cycles in cooperation with embassies, cultural institutions or civic organizations and, when possible, with the participation of the scriptwriter, director or performers. Since 1984, it has mounted a yearly, non-competitive film festival which has brought many quality films and video productions to the country. Educational courses offered for adults are well attended, and programs with Jerusalem schoolchildren encourage critical analysis of a popular medium.

Cultural life in the Arab sector, both within the framework of the community itself and as part of the country's cultural mainstream, expresses the Arab population's affinity to the Arab world as a whole and its status as a minority group in Israel. In the early years of the state, the works of Arab authors and poets were characterized by local, rural subjects popular in the conservative, semi-closed society of those days; contemporary literature incorporates traditional Arab influences with modern Western trends. Arabic prose and poetry is translated into Hebrew, and Hebrew writings appear in Arabic translation either in book form or in one of several flourishing literary magazines. Music, theater, dance and art focus on creative activities which tend to integrate popular folklore traditions with various Islamic and Western art forms.

A number of Arab authors (Anton Shammas, Michel Haddad, Emile Habibi) and actors (Muhammad Bakri, Yusuf Abu Varda and Mauhram Khoury) have achieved prominence among the Israeli public, and performances by mixed Arab-Jewish folk dance and music ensembles draw enthusiastic audiences. A 1994 production of "Romeo and Juliet" by a troupe of Jewish and Arab actors from Jerusalem, performing in a mixture of Hebrew and Arabic, met with national and international acclaim and has toured widely abroad. Arabs take an active part in the country's electronic media as producers, editors, announcers, commentators and performers, both in general radio and television as well as in Arabic programming.

As in the country's other ethnic sectors, Arab cultural activities and preservation of the Arab cultural heritage are encouraged by various government and voluntary agencies which offer assistance, ranging from grants to writers and artists to providing support for museums and cultural centers.

LIGHT ENTERTAINMENT

The concept of 'popular' entertainment began in Israel during the 1940s with such groups as *Chizbatron, Matateh* and *Batzal Yarok*. However the major impetus occurred during the 1960s with the formation of entertainment troupes attached to different military units. Among the country's leading entertainers who began their careers during their army service are Haim Topol, Si Hyman, Miri Aloni, Dorit Reuveni and Yardena Arazi. While television and radio are the main mediums for popular entertainment, live performances by comedians, singers, musicians, bands and groups take place regularly throughout the country.

Some vocalists have achieved perennial stardom such as Arik Einstein, Shlomo Artzi, Matti Caspi, Shalom Hanoch and Yehudit Ravitz, as have some bands, including *Kaveret, Mashina, Atraf, Etnix*, and *Haverim shel Natasha*. Some artists are also popular abroad, including the veterans Shoshana Damari and Yaffa Yarkoni, and a new generation such as Dudu Fisher, Ofra Haza, Rami Kleinstein, Aviv Gefen, David Broza, Ahinoam Nini and the mime artist, Hanoch Rosenn.

Grand-scale musicals in Hebrew translation, including "Les Miserables" and "The Sound of Music," which were popular in Israel in the 1970s, have recently been revived to enthusiastic acclaim.

Increasingly popular among Israelis of Sephardic backgrounds is an Eastern musical genre deriving primarily from Arabic and Greek influences, as performed by singers such as Haim Moshe, Eli Luzon, Shimi Tavori, Boaz Sha'arabi, Margalit Tsa'anani, Zehava Ben (who specializes in the songs of the legendary Umm Kulthum) and Ofer Levy.

In the field of comedy, the *Gashash Hahiver* trio have been performing for decades and are still unchallenged at the top, although a new generation of stand-up comics are beginning to command substantial followings. Television personalities with very popular shows of their own include Dudu Topaz, Gidi Gov, Meni Pe'er, Dan Margalit, Dan Shilon, Ilana Dayan and Rivka Michaeli.

MEDIA

Keeping informed of events in Israel, the Middle East and the world in general, is very important to Israelis. Listening to hourly radio bulletins, viewing television news broadcasts and reading at least one daily newspaper are part of most Israelis' daily routine.

Israel's commitment to freedom of the press applies to all communications media, with only security matters subject to censorship. A dozen Hebrew newspapers and several in other languages appear regularly, as well as more than 1,000 periodicals, many of which are magazines for special interest groups.

RADIO AND TELEVISION

Kol Israel (Voice of Israel) operates eight radio networks which offer programming in 17 languages, ranging from light entertainment and popular music to academic lectures, panel discussions and classical music, each geared to a different audience, from children to seniors, from newcomers to veteran Israelis. *Galei Tzahal* (station of the Israel Defense Forces) broadcasts around the clock, featuring news and music as well as programs of special interest to soldiers. Multilingual, short-wave transmissions for listeners abroad provide a constant and reliable source of informa-

tion about Israel, the Middle East and Jewish affairs.

Television began in Israel in 1967; today this state-run channel, on the air from 6:30 A.M. to 1:00 A.M., offers educational, information and entertainment programming in Hebrew, Arabic and English. One local commercial channel, inaugurated in 1994, is divided among three private producers, with certain hours reserved daily for educational programs. Cable television, funded by monthly subscription fees, is now available in most of the country, making it possible to receive American, European and Asian networks. Independent Israeli cable channels present sports, children's features, movies and documentaries.

Kol Israel and the state-run television channel operate under the aegis of the Israeli Broadcasting Authority (IBA), which is subject to the IBA Law (1965) defining broadcasting as an independent government service, charged with giving expression to diverse perspectives. The IBA is headed by an executive committee, appointed by the government for a three-year term, and by a director-general, appointed for a five-year term. IBA broadcasting is financed by advertising on radio, public service announcements, and an annual fee paid by consumers.

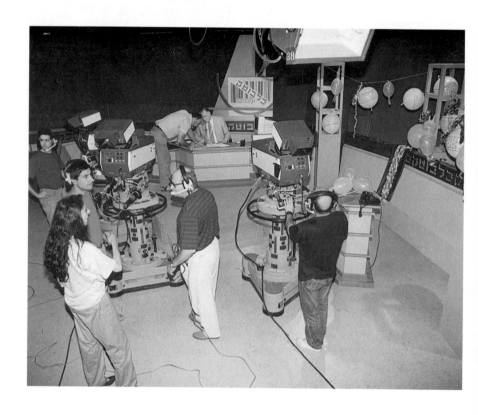

Singers from around the world at the biennial Zimriya festival

Israel's international cultural ties focus on cooperation in a broad range of fields, including language, literature, the arts, science, media and sports. Based on cultural agreements with more than 70 countries, in addition to links with many others, activities range from student and academic exchange programs and reciprocal tours by dance troupes, theater companies, art exhibits, musicians and orchestras, to participation in book fairs, film festivals and sports competitions as well as the teaching of the language and cultural traditions of both countries.

ARIEL is Israel's leading cultural magazine. It has been published since 1962 and gives extensive coverage to all fields of the arts and literature in Israel – prose and poetry, cinema, dance, painting and sculpture, music, archaeology, architecture and literary criticism. Its contributors include Israel's leading men and women of letters and the arts and academic figures.

Ariel is published quarterly in English, French, German, Spanish, Arabic and Russian editions. Readers who wish to keep abreast of Israel's cultural scene will find it an invaluable source of information. Interested subscribers should apply to Israel's diplomatic missions abroad.

israel among the nations

NORTH AMERICA

LATIN AMERICA

EUROPE

AFRICA

ASIA AND THE PACIFIC

ARAB COUNTRIES

THE HOLY SEE

INTERNATIONAL COOPERATION

UNITED NATIONS

WORLD JEWRY

ISRAEL AMONG THE NATIONS

אדיר חפצה של ישראל
לקיים יחסים תקינים
עם כל המדינות,
עם ממשלותיהן ועם עמיהן...
(דוד בן-גוריון, תשי"ג)

It is Israel's fervent wish
to maintain good relations
with all countries,
with their governments
and their peoples...
(David Ben-Gurion, 1952)

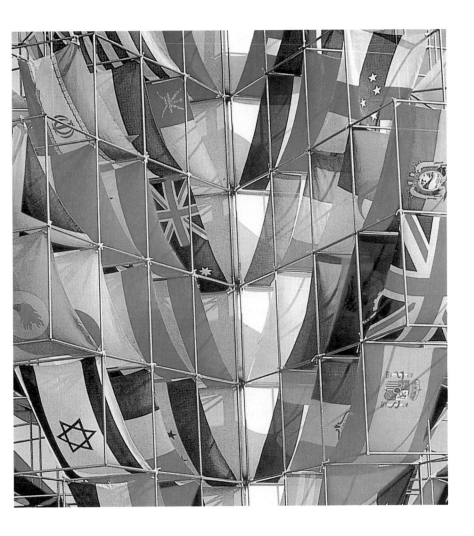

The State of Israel, a member of the United Nations since 1949, maintains relations with the majority of countries around the world. With memories of centuries of persecution, the shattering experience of the Holocaust and the decades-long Arab-Israeli conflict, Israel's foreign policy has been geared to advance peace in the region while ensuring the country's security and promoting cooperation with all nations.

NORTH AMERICA

UNITED STATES

Eleven minutes after the proclamation of Israel's independence on 14 May 1948, American President Harry S. Truman extended recognition to the new state. This act marked the beginning of a relationship based on common values and characterized by deep friendship and mutual respect. Both countries are vibrant democracies whose political and legal systems are anchored in liberal traditions; both began as pioneer societies; and both are still receiving and integrating new immigrants. At times the two countries have 'agreed to disagree.' When differences do arise, they generally stem from the conflict between the United States' position as a superpower with complex global interests and Israel's primary concern, as a small state in a turbulent region, of preservation of its sovereignty and security.

At the same time that the United States was beginning to develop its diplomatic and political relations with Israel, it also joined other Western countries in an arms embargo to the Middle East, believing that by so doing regional tensions would be significantly reduced. After 1952, the Eisenhower administration's pursuit of Arab support for a Middle East security pact foreshadowed a radical departure from the Truman administration's partiality towards Israel. Relations between Washington and Jerusalem only drew closer again in the late 1950s following American disillusionment with Egyptian President Gamal Abdel Nasser's policies. During the Kennedy administration, the previous American policy on arms supplies was reversed with the lifting of the existing embargo.

Since the latter part of the Johnson administration (late 1960s), American diplomacy has been based on a commitment to Israel's right to exist within secure and recognized boundaries to be achieved through direct negotiations with its Arab neighbors. Believing that a strong Israel is a sine qua non for attaining peace in the region, the United States committed itself to maintaining Israel's qualitative edge over Arab armies. During the Nixon and Carter administrations, it assisted in concluding disengagement agreements between Israel and Egypt and Israel and Syria (1973-74), the Camp David Accords (1978) and the Egypt–Israel Peace Treaty (1979).

During the Reagan administration, relations not only flourished, but were also given a more formal and concrete content. In addition to previous commitments, memorandums of understanding were signed (1981, 1988), forming the basis for setting up a number of joint planning and consultative bodies, which in turn generated practical arrangements in both military and civilian fields. These frameworks of mutual cooperation were subsequently codified in a wider memorandum (1988). The Bush administration endorsed Israel's peace initiative (1989) and co-sponsored the Madrid Peace Conference (1991) which led to the convening of peace talks in Washington, D.C.

The Clinton administration has played a key role in the Middle East peace process by actively supporting the agreements between Israel and the Palestinians, Israel's peace treaty with Jordan, negotiations with Syria and efforts to promote regional cooperation, including an end to the Arab boycott. Pledging to maintain Israel's qualitative edge, it has also committed itself to minimizing the security risks that Israel might incur in its pursuit of peace. Moreover, the

President Clinton and Prime Minister Netanyahu

United States has recently taken several important measures to back Israel in its war against terrorism.

The continuing and deepening amity between Israel and the United States has been defined by various American administrations in terms ranging from the preservation of Israel as a 'basic tenet' of American foreign policy, with emphasis on a 'special relationship' between the two states, to a declaration of an 'American commitment' to Israel. By the early 1980s, Israel was regarded by the United States as a 'strategic asset' and was designated (1987), in accordance with legislation passed the previous year, as a 'major non-NATO ally.' Congressional backing for Israel is bipartisan. Support for annual military and economic assistance, the peace process and Israel's struggle against terrorism have been hallmarks of Congress' commitment to United States–Israel friendship, as was the passage of legislation (1995) recognizing Jerusalem as the united capital of Israel and calling for the establishment of the United States embassy in Jerusalem by May 1999.

The 'special relationship' encompasses mutual economic, political, strategic and diplomatic concerns. Israel currently receives some $3 billion a year in security and economic aid, and bilateral trade has been enhanced by the Israel–United States Free Trade Area Agreement (1985). A growing number of joint ventures sponsored by Israeli and American industrial firms have been established, and several American states have entered into 'state-to-state' agreements with Israel, involving activities ranging from culture to agriculture.

The United States usually stands by Israel's side in international forums, staving off attempts both in the United Nations (UN) and in associated bodies to push through anti-Israel resolutions. The two countries have been cooperating to their mutual advantage in exchanges of intelligence and military information, as well as in the war against international terror and the campaign against drugs. United States–Israel friendship is bolstered by a supportive Jewish community and a wide segment of American society.

CANADA

Canada and Israel have had full diplomatic relations for many years, based on common democratic values, with bilateral links enhanced by cultural and scientific exchanges. In the international arena, Canada's support for Israel is expressed through its generally pro-Israel stance in various UN forums.

LATIN AMERICA

In the UN General Assembly vote (29 November 1947) on the resolution which proposed establishing two states, one Jewish and one Arab, on the territory included in the British Mandate for Palestine, 13 of the 20 Latin American member nations voted in favor of partition.

Soon after Israel achieved independence (May 1948), close ties were developed with the countries of Latin America. Today, 32 out of the 33 countries of Central and South America and the Caribbean region maintain full diplomatic relations with Israel.

In the 1950s and 1960s, relations were strengthened due in no small measure to joint cooperation programs in which Israel shared its experience and skills in various areas relevant to Latin America such as agriculture, medicine, organization of cooperatives and rural, regional and community development. Thousands of Latin Americans participated in study programs in Israel, and many Israeli experts worked on development projects in Latin America. Expanded in the 1970s to include the newly-independent states in the Caribbean, this dialogue for development still continues today.

Local and international political developments during the 1960s and 1970s led to a lessening of support for Israel among the countries of Latin America and the Caribbean, which since then has been apparent mainly at the UN and its affiliated bodies. Bilateral relations are generally friendly, with frequent reciprocal visits by heads of state, ministers, parliamentary delegations, prominent clergy, trade union leaders and mayors.

Exports, including chemicals, agricultural produce, machinery and electronics, and imports, consisting mainly of meat, grain, corn, sugar, cocoa, coffee and metals, are both on the increase, and Israeli banks, construction firms and agricultural planning and development companies are active in Latin America. Cultural and scientific agreements for the exchange of artists, students and athletes, as well as television and radio programs, operative with some 20 countries, are coordinated by the Institute of Israel - Iberoamerican Culture in Jerusalem.

EUROPE

Similar systems of government and shared social values, as well as the long and sometimes tragic history of Jewish communities in Europe, form the foundation of relations between Israel and the European countries. Each bilateral relationship is expressed in a wide range of economic, cultural, scientific, technological and political activities, as well as by ongoing dialogues maintained with heads of state, ministers, parliamentarians and public figures through frequent reciprocal visits.

WESTERN EUROPE

Since economic relations with neighboring Arab countries are just beginning, Western Europe is Israel's most natural trading partner. The establishment of a free trade zone (1975) with the European Community (EC) led to a significant increase in exports to Europe from 1975 to 1996, and an even greater increase in EC exports to Israel. This growth in trade has been accelerated by the development of close business connections between entrepreneurs and investors and the setting up of joint ventures, as well as by efforts to strengthen economic ties with the member countries of the European Free Trade Association (EFTA). In 1995, Israel and the EU (European Union) concluded a broader agreement which expresses even closer ties. The flow of tourists between Europe and Israel has established an ever-deepening fabric of personal relationships and mutual awareness.

The Western European countries support the effort to resolve the Arab-Israel conflict through the ongoing peace process.

EASTERN EUROPE

Relations between Israel and the countries of Central and Eastern Europe, which were renewed as soon as the area was freed from Soviet control, are becoming increasingly close, especially in economic matters, culture, tourism and international cooperation activities. Economic agreements with these countries are of importance given that many of them are candidates for future membership in the European Union and NATO.

As these countries had been the center of world Jewry before World War II, the memory of the Holocaust is a significant factor in relations with them. Issues being dealt with include restoration of nationalized Jewish public and private property to their owners or legal heirs and recognition of the 'Righteous Gentiles' who risked their lives to save Jews during the Nazi era.

Israel's relations with Russia and the Commonwealth of Independent States (CIS) have gained momentum in recent years, as evidenced by Russia's participation in aspects of the Middle East peace process. Relations with the Muslim countries of the CIS (Azerbaijan, Kazakhstan, Kyrgyzstan, Turkmenistan, Uzbekistan and Tadjikistan) have been established. The leaders of several of these countries have visited Israel and signed mutual cooperation agreements, and economic ties are becoming closer.

Parallel to diplomatic relations, special relations are also emerging with Israel's large community of recent immigrants from former Soviet countries, leading to the establishment of enhanced cultural and economic ties. At the same time, Jewish immigration to Israel is continuing.

Minister of Foreign Affairs Javier Solana of Spain and Minister of Foreign Affairs Shimon Peres, signing the Treaty of Association between Israel and the EU, 1995

AFRICA

Ties with Black African states began in the mid-1950s, even before some of them achieved independence. Contacts with Ghana were the first (1956), and from then on diplomatic, commercial, cultural and technical assistance links expanded until they encompassed most of the countries south of the Sahara. These ties expressed an affinity with Israel, itself a young state, which had become independent less than a decade before (1948) and was eager to share its experience with the new African states. In the late 1960s and early 1970s, Israel maintained full diplomatic relations with 33 Black African countries. Mutually beneficial economic ties were also established, including a number of joint ventures.

In the aftermath of the 1973 oil crisis, most of the Black African states severed diplomatic ties with Israel, due to Arab promises of cheap oil and financial aid and in compliance with the OAU resolution, sponsored by Egypt, to sever relations with Israel. Full diplomatic ties were continued only by Malawi, Lesotho and Swaziland, while a few other countries maintained their links through Israeli interest offices at foreign embassies. Commercial ties were also not entirely disrupted, many Black African students continued to train in Israel and Israeli experts were active in Black Africa.

Since the 1980s, diplomatic relations with Black African countries have been gradually renewed, gaining momentum with the ongoing peace negotiations between Israel and its Arab neighbors. Today, 40 African countries maintain diplomatic ties with Israel, and reciprocal visits by heads of state and government ministers take place frequently. In May 1994, Israel's President Ezer Weizman attended the historic inauguration of Nelson Mandela as the first Black African president of South Africa.

President Mandela of South Africa and President Weizman

ASIA AND THE PACIFIC

Israel maintains diplomatic relations with most Asian states. The growing economic and political strength of these countries, as well as the ongoing peace process in the Middle East, have contributed to the intensification of ties in the political, cultural and, above all, economic spheres. Technical cooperation with Israel in the areas of rural development, agriculture and education has also played an important role in relations with the developing countries of the region.

During 1991-92, Israel established diplomatic relations with China, India and Mongolia and, in 1993, with Vietnam, Cambodia and Laos, leading to enhanced cooperation in various fields. Since the mid-1980s, Israel and Japan have steadily expanded bilateral cooperation, reflected *inter alia* in the signing of several agreements, reciprocal visits of prime ministers and ministers and Japan's contribution to the multilateral peace process. Israel has had full diplomatic ties with Australia and New Zealand for many years. In the recent past, relations have been established with ten newly independent island states, most of which participate in Israel's various programs of international cooperation.

Prime Minister Li Peng of China and Minister of Foreign Affairs David Levy

ARAB COUNTRIES
EGYPT

Israel and Egypt signed a peace treaty in 1979, marking the end of 30 years of relentless hostility and five costly wars. The treaty was preceded by Egyptian President Anwar Sadat's visit to Jerusalem (1977), at the invitation of Israel's Prime Minister Menachem Begin, as well as the signing of the Camp David Accords (1978) which constituted a basis for peace between Egypt and Israel and between Israel and its other neighbors. The accords also addressed the need to solve the Palestinian issue, following a five-year interim phase of autonomy for the Palestinian Arab residents of Judea and Samaria (the West Bank) and the Gaza Strip. President Sadat and Prime

Minister Begin were jointly awarded the Nobel Peace Prize for their achievement.

The peace implemented between Israel and Egypt consists of several major elements, including the termination of the state of war as well as acts or threats of belligerency, hostility or violence; the establishment of diplomatic, economic and cultural ties; the removal of barriers to trade and freedom of movement; and withdrawal by Israel from the Sinai peninsula, with agreed security arrangements and limited force zones. Israel completed its withdrawal from the Sinai (1982) according to the terms of the treaty, giving up strategic military bases and other assets in exchange for peace.

Although Egypt was ostracized by other Arab states following the signing of the treaty, most have since reestablished relations with Egypt and reopened their embassies in Cairo. The headquarters of the Arab League, which had been transferred to Tunis, were reinstated in Cairo in the early 1980s.

Having to overcome 30 years of distrust and hostility, normalization of relations between Israel and Egypt is a long and arduous process. Yet, embassies and consulates have been established by both countries, and meetings between government ministers and high-ranking officials take place regularly. Reciprocal visits of businessmen and experts in various fields have also become common-

place. Airline and bus routes operate daily between the two countries, and a decision to establish a permanent joint committee for the development of tourism has been reached. Scientific cooperation includes marine agriculture technology, development of environmental protection resources, cancer research and joint projects on the prevention of pollution in the Gulf of Eilat. Agricultural cooperation is growing steadily; in 1995 alone more than 700 farmers from Egypt took part in courses on agricultural subjects in Israel and 'on-the-spot' courses by Israeli experts in Egypt were attended by 300 participants.

As the first state to sign a peace treaty with Israel, Egypt assists in the ongoing negotiations between Israel and the Palestinians.

King Hussein of Jordan and the late Prime Minister Rabin

JORDAN

The peace treaty between Jordan and Israel, signed at the Akaba-Eilat border crossing (October 1994), was preceded by a meeting of King Hussein and Prime Minister Yitzhak Rabin in Washington three months earlier when the two leaders proclaimed an end to the state of war between their countries.

Although *de facto* at war with each other for 46 years, Israel and Jordan had maintained secret contacts and concluded mutually beneficial agreements throughout that entire period. The 1991 Madrid Conference led to public bilateral talks, culminating in a formal treaty (1994) in which both countries have undertaken to refrain from acts of belligerency, to ensure that no threats of violence to the other will originate within their territory, to endeavor to prevent terrorism and act together to achieve security and cooperation in the Middle East by replacing military preparedness with confidence-building measures. Other provisions include agreed allocations from existing water resources, freedom of passage for nationals of both countries, efforts to alleviate the refugee problem and cooperation in the development of the Jordan Rift Valley. The international boundary delineated in the treaty has replaced the 1949 cease-fire lines and is delimited with reference to the British Mandate boundary (1922-48).

With the ratification of the peace treaty, full diplomatic relations were established and, since then, the relationship between Israel and Jordan has been moving forward steadily. The Jordanian parliament's decision (August 1995) to rescind its adherence to the Arab boycott of Israel, as well as the regional economic conference held in Amman (November 1995), serve as positive indicators for the future, and the open border crossings between the two countries have facilitated normalization of relations. Joint business ventures are being initiated, reciprocal tourism is steadily increasing and the free movement of business people by both land and air has brought about an atmosphere of open communication and cooperation.

The basis for implementation of the Israel-Jordan peace treaty was established with the signing and ratification of 15 bilateral agreements in economic, scientific and cultural spheres. These treaties are to serve as the foundation of peaceful, normal relations between Israel and the Hashemite Kingdom of Jordan.

Israel Defense Forces saluting the Jordanian army as it plays the national anthems of both countries

MAGHREB COUNTRIES

Since 1994, three North African Arab states – Morocco, Mauritania and Tunisia – have joined other Arab countries and chosen to take the path of peace and reconciliation by forming diplomatic ties with Israel.

Initiated in different ways at various levels, relations between Morocco and Israel were formalized when Israel opened a liaison office (November 1994) in the Moroccan capital, Rabat. Four months later, Morocco opened its office in Israel, thus formally establishing bilateral diplomatic relations.

The Islamic Republic of Mauritania and Israel concluded an agreement at the Barcelona Conference (November 1995), in the presence of the Spanish foreign minister, to establish interest sections in the Spanish embassies in Tel Aviv and Nauakchoff (the Mauritanian capital), respectively. Mauritania opened its diplomatic mission in Tel Aviv (May 1996) and indicated its wish to fully normalize relations with Israel.

Following a timetable worked out by Israel, Tunisia and the United States (January 1996), Israel opened an interest office in Tunisia (April 1996), and Tunisia reciprocated six weeks later (May 1996).

Diplomatic relations with the Maghreb countries are especially important because of Israel's large population of North African emigrés who retain an emotional attachment to the countries where their families lived for many centuries. This affinity is an asset which may lead to more profound relationships and make a practical contribution to the peace process.

GULF STATES

As a result of the ongoing peace process in the Middle East, the Gulf States have shown interest in relations with Israel for the first time since 1948. Initial contacts were followed with a series of reciprocal visits by high-level officials. In May 1996, Israel opened a trade representation office in Oman to develop economic, scientific and trade relations, with emphasis on water resources utilization, tourism, agriculture, chemicals and advanced technologies, while Oman opened an office in Tel Aviv in August 1996. In May 1996, Israel set up a trade representation office in Qatar to facilitate development of an ongoing economic and commercial relationship. Qatar is expected to open a similar office in Israel to promote mutually beneficial activities and projects.

THE HOLY SEE

The establishment of full diplomatic relations between Israel and the Holy See (under the terms of a Fundamental Agreement signed in Jerusalem in December 1993) will surely be viewed as a step of major significance in a historic process of change in the Church's attitude to Judaism and the Jewish people, whose public initiation can be attributed to the declaration known as *Nostra Aetate*, issued by the Second Vatican Council in 1965.

In their Fundamental Agreement, Israel and the Holy See noted the *"unique nature of the relationship between the Catholic Church and the Jewish people..."* and committed themselves to *"appropriate cooperation in* *combating all forms of antisemitism and all kinds of racism and religious intolerance, and in promoting mutual understanding among nations, tolerance among communities and respect for human life and dignity,"* and *"the peaceful resolution of conflicts among states and nations, excluding violence and terror from international life."* Other obligations of the respective parties concern the *Status Quo* regime affecting the Christian Holy Places, protection of Catholic sacred places, questions relating to freedom of religion, religious study, education, the functioning of Catholic church institutions in Israel, pilgrimage to the Holy Land and other matters arising in their general context.

The signing of the Fundamental Agreement, December 1993

INTERNATIONAL COOPERATION: MEETING THE CHALLENGE

Since its establishment (1948), Israel has expressed eagerness to share with the international community skills learned from its own development experience: overcoming harsh climatic conditions, inadequate water resources, desertification, disease and epidemics, and finding solutions to socio-economic problems. This desire led to the founding (1958) of MASHAV – The Center for International Cooperation – within the Ministry of Foreign Affairs. In cooperation with other government ministries and professional and academic institutions throughout Israel, MASHAV offers training programs for participants from developing countries all over the world designed to enhance professional skills by combining theory with a hands-on approach, by integrating research with project implementation and imparting concepts and ideas to be adapted as on-site solutions to meet the priorities of developing countries.

Since MASHAV's inception, over 50,000 men and women from as far away as Mongolia and as close as the Palestinian Authority have taken part in MASHAV courses in Israel; almost 70,000 trainees have participated in on-the-spot courses abroad; and over 10,000 long- and short-term consultants have been sent to assist in the design and implementation of development projects throughout the world. MASHAV is currently cooperating with 141 countries, authorities and international agencies to promote technical cooperation programs in various fields. Cooperation efforts include countries in Africa, Asia, the Commonwealth of Independent States and Latin America.

Since the Middle East Peace Conference in Madrid (1991), MASHAV has made the broadening and strengthening of regional cooperation a priority. As the peace process gains momentum, MASHAV's activities will reach more countries, thus contributing its expertise to meet the challenges of the coming century.

UNITED NATIONS

The State of Israel was admitted to the United Nations (UN) as its 59th member on 11 May 1949. Since then, it has participated in a wide range of UN operations and has endeavored to make its full contribution to UN organizations dealing with health, labor, food and agriculture, education and science. Israel plays an active role in the work of non-governmental organizations, conducted under UN auspices, which deal with issues ranging from aviation to immigration, from communications to meteorology, from trade to the status of women.

Some UN resolutions have been of crucial significance for Israel, among them Security Council Resolutions 242 (22 November 1967) and 338 (22 October 1973), providing an agreed framework for settling the Arab-Israel dispute.

Over the years, the UN has been active in bringing about a cessation of hostilities between Israel and its Arab neighbors by appointing mediators, extending UN auspices to cease-fire and armistice agreements and stationing UN forces between the adversaries.

At the same time, the UN was used for years as a battleground for political warfare against Israel. The 21 Arab states, with the aid of Islamic countries, the non-aligned camp and the former Communist bloc, constituted an 'automatic majority', assuring the adoption of anti-Israel resolutions in the General Assembly.

Since the end of the Cold War and the momentum gained in the Middle East peace process, a somewhat more balanced approach is evident in General Assembly resolutions regarding the Middle East. Recently, Israel has also increased its involvement in United Nations activities around the world.

Israel Day Parade, New York

WORLD JEWRY

Since the first exile (586 BCE) and subsequent dispersions of Jews throughout the world, a unique and dynamic relationship has existed between Jews living in the Land of Israel and those residing outside it. Although separated by long distances over many centuries, the Jews have remained one nation, bound by a common history, religion and homeland as well as a collective commitment to the physical and spiritual survival of the Jewish people. The establishment of the State of Israel (1948) grew out of their 2,000-year-old dream to return to their ancestral homeland and revive its national life and sovereignty.

Recent estimates put the world Jewish population at about 13 million, 34 percent of whom live in Israel, some 50 percent in North and South America, 15 percent in Europe and the rest in other places, mainly in South Africa and Australia. Jews everywhere share a spectrum of symbols and behavior, and are engaged in ongoing dialogue on a wide range of issues.

Diaspora Jews, in recognition of the centrality of Israel in Jewish life, participate in building the country through financial contributions, social and political support, and, in some cases, by coming to Israel to live, adding their particular skills and cultural backgrounds to the Israeli mosaic. A long tradition of mutual aid among Jews is manifested today in a multi-faceted network of organizations dedicated to hundreds of Jewish-Israeli interests. For its part, Israel seeks to strengthen Diaspora Jewish communities and its ties with them by promoting Israel-oriented activities, Hebrew language study, financial investment, joint economic ventures and visits by groups, individuals and study missions.

World Zionist Organization (WZO) was founded at the First Zionist Congress (1897) with the aim of facilitating the return of the Jewish people to its ancient homeland, the Land of Israel, and reviving Jewish national life in the country. The WZO's primary objective was attained in 1948 with the establishment of a legally secured, internationally recognized Jewish state – the State of Israel. Since then the WZO has functioned as liaison to Diaspora Jewry, promoting activities which focus on the unity of the Jewish people and the centrality of Israel in Jewish life; facilitating immigration; fostering Jewish education in Jewish communities worldwide; and defending the rights of Jews wherever they live. The democratically-elected World Zionist Congress, the supreme body of the WZO, meets every 4-5 years in Jerusalem to legislate, determine financial policy and elect its executive committee.

 Jewish Agency for Israel (JAFI) is today a primary organizational expression of the relationship between the State of Israel and world Jewry. It was constituted (1929) by the World Zionist Organization to represent the Jewish community in the Land of Israel vis-a-vis the British Mandate authorities, foreign governments and international organizations. After Israel attained independence, partial responsibility for certain national tasks were delegated by law to JAFI and the WZO, including immigration and absorption, rural settlement and immigrant housing, educational and youth activities, as well as urban renewal. In recent years, many of these functions have been assumed by the government.

 JAFI and WZO budgets derive mainly from funds raised by the United Jewish Appeal (UJA) in the United States and by Keren Heyesod (KH) in the rest of the world. Half of JAFI's governing bodies – the Board of Governors, which convenes three times a year, and the Assembly, which meets annually in Jerusalem – are comprised of members of the WZO (according to party representation), while the other half represents the UJA (30 percent) and KH (20 percent).

ISRAEL INFORMATION CENTER

Edited by Ellen Hirsch
Design - Cover, Chapter Dividers and Table of Contents: Naomi Morag
Typesetting: Youval Tal Ltd.
Color Separations and Plates by Art Plus

Statistics: Central Bureau of Statistics, Bank of Israel and UNESCO
Economy chapter: Text by Moshe Felber
Map of Israel: Atir Ltd., Rehovot

Photographs:
Albatross, R. Alkabetz, ASAP, S. Avnisan, A. Avrahami, W. Braun, V. Etzion,
S. Ginott, J. Golan, M. Haramaty, A. Hirschfield, E. Hool, Image Bank,
E. Klagsbrun, M. Koren, Y. Loeff, J. Malcolm, R. Milon, Dan-Nataf, J. Seraro,
M. Shamir, N. Shorer, E. Simanor, F. Sklar, S. Zakai

Thanks for photographs to: AZYF, Government Press Office, Israel Aircraft
Industries, Israel Museum, Israel Nature Reserve Authority, Jewish National
Fund, Ministry of Industry and Trade, Ministry of the Environment, Ministry
of Tourism, Ophir Optronics, Weizmann Institute

Ilustrations: A. Berg, R. Etgar, Gretty

Printed by Hamakor Press
Jerusalem, Israel, 1996